The GRUDGE DITCH GANG

(A Novel of Memoirs on Growing Up in the 1960s Mississippi Delta)

Jessie Haynes

Library or Congress U.S. Copyright Data:

Registration #: TXu-001803975

ISBN: 978-0-9702069-2-3

www.jessiehaynesbooks.com

Cover design & book layout by Looks Good on Paper

Table of Contents

About the Author

Jessie Haynes is a writer who grew up in the Mississippi Delta with her 12 siblings. Her life was infused with the colorful community that included living a block away from the renowned "Hole in the Wall" nightclub that hosted so many of America's famed blues singers. As a child, she sat at the feet of one of America's most well-known women in the civil rights effort – Fannie Lou Hamer.

After living stints in Illinois, California, Pennsylvania and Virginia, Jessie now resides in Southeast Texas. She is a former publisher of two travel magazines, three social magazines and three business directories. The former news reporter for Mississippi's "Delta Democrat-Times Newspaper," university relations executive director and chief executive officer of a regional public relations firm currently works in education. Her first book, "10 Stupid Things College Kids Do," is a self-help guide for first generation college freshmen. The self-published book has sold more than 20,000 copies since its debut in 2000. Her second book, for which she served as a ghost writer, sold out at 10,000 copies in just a few months. She has hosted several local government cable and web TV shows and appeared briefly on *The Oprah Winfrey Show*, the *700 Club*, *The Peoples Court* and a number of market specific news/feature shows.

Since completing "The Grudge Ditch Gang," Jessie has vowed to finish and already returned to work on her next book, "Diary of a PR Woman." She expects to complete it in the coming year and then return to her manuscript that represents part two of "The Grudge Ditch Gang." The second part covers the teen years of Jessie's life as she navigates another whole phase of growing up on the Low End of Cleveland's Mississippi Delta.

Foreword

If you liked *The Help*, were inspired by *The Color Purple* or appreciated *Adventures of Huckleberry Finn*, you will love *The Grudge Ditch Gang*. From sitting on the morning bench and hunting wild hogs to making homebrew for some of the famed Hole in the Wall nightclub patrons or sitting at the feet of Fannie Lou Hamer, this colorful memoir of young Jessie highlights the childhood of the author as she grew up in the Mississippi Delta. "The Grudge Ditch Gang" weaves together a community's effort to raise its children in the face of poverty and politics that attempt to keep basic government services as sanitation, streets and water from Jessie's family and their neighbors.

The humor, struggles and successes are told through the eyes of a young girl who grows up wrapped in the love and protection of her parents, 12 siblings and the other surrounding large families who carved a neighborhood in the "Low End" of this small Mississippi Delta town. Their community's nemesis gave the children their uncoveted name of the Grudge Ditch Gang.

Prepare yourself for laughter, tears, joy, pain and a story that makes many of us envy young Jessie's economically impoverished life that was rich with the love of family and community.

– Lester Brown, Author of "Power in Belief"

Dedication

This book is dedicated to my daughters Tameka and Raven and to my granddaughter Coy.

Also, may my many nieces and nephews and their children and grandchildren cherish these stories as part of our family's interesting history.

Note

"The Grudge Ditch Gang" represents my childhood memories and in no way intends to hurt anyone's feelings, malign anyone's name, exclude anyone or misrepresent the facts. It is simply my story as I remember the events that impacted my world.

A few names have been changed to protect the guilty.

From the City to the Country

For the first seven years of my life, we lived in the city – a metropolis that was all of 15,000 people! As far back as I can remember, the main industry in Cleveland, Mississippi, has always been cotton. The agribusiness of cotton, Delta State College, now a university, the public schools, and Baxter's Laboratory were and are still the top employers in town.

Daddy drove 18-wheeler Mack trucks across the country to pick up loads of beer for two distribution companies – Hawkins and Wells. Falstaff and several sister beers were distributed by the Hawkins. The Wells family distributed Schlitz Malt Liquor and its relative beers. The two companies kept Daddy on the road for at least four days a week. New Orleans, Memphis,

Milwaukee, Houston, Richmond, Chicago and other cities were on his itinerary as he trekked across America. It was a big deal for us when Daddy would go on a short trip and take one or two of us children traveling with him in what seemed like a house on wheels.

On other days, many evenings and even early mornings before or after a trip, Daddy was busy as a mechanic. His gas station/mechanic shop was located on Ruby Street, next door to St. Peter's Rock Church. Daddy and Uncle Louie were partners in the business, with Uncle Louie focusing on the gas station and Daddy taking care of the automotive maintenance and repair work. My father, L.D. Haynes, was unequivocally the best mechanic in the Delta. The area high schools and the colleges recruited him to teach on their campuses. He said thanks, but no thanks, and continued to work on the 18-wheelers he drove across country for the Hawkins, the Wells and others who had heard of his work.

People lined up their jalopies – cars, trucks and tractors – for him to fix a carburetor, motor, transmission, alternator, universal joint or some other ailing part of their vehicles. Frankly, Daddy just loved working. When he wasn't driving trucks or repairing automobiles, he was deejaying on Saturday nights in the nearby nightclubs where his fans called him Dr. Soul. Sometimes the club owners paid him and sometimes he worked for the joy of just helping out the club owners.

I can't began to tell you how many people never paid him for the hours he spent making sure their automobiles drove smoothly or the many hours he would spin records and jive talk to entertain and educate the patrons who swayed to the music booming from the five-foot tall, black screened speaker boxes that he personally built. In fact, the Peavey speakers with their big woofers and high wattages, made in Greenwood, Mississippi, just down the road from Cleveland, couldn't compete with my Daddy's masterpieces of sound. Partygoers often bragged that Dr. Soul's music blew the roof off the clubs and could have been inspiration for a later best selling song by the group Parliament – "Give up the Funk, Tear the Roof off the Sucker."

For sure, my siblings and I felt our home shake many times as Daddy tested the sounds of his musical line up from his office in the back of our home. The sound waves appeared to move the walls and lift the ceiling as Daddy tested new heights of decibels. While Daddy didn't mass produce his speakers as Peavey did, he made speakers for several of his musician friends, especially the blues singers from around the Delta who often graced Daddy's office as they picked and plucked sounds of woe, pain and unrequited love on their guitars and recorded on a massive reel to reel tape machine.

My mother complained that Daddy needed to fix, build or do things for his family instead of for everyone else. That nagging was probably part of what drove Daddy to buying five acres of land in the Southern tip of town – called the Low End. Daddy and my older brothers cleared the land and prepared it for the house they would build with their own hands. The house would have two full bathrooms, a family room, four bedrooms, a full-size kitchen, a laundry room and more. This dream home would be almost three times the size of our home in the city. A swimming pool and lots of land for us to explore were part of Daddy's plans that kept us excited about our move.

The Low End home would be so unlike our little five-room, white wood-frame house with its screened front porch that was not only home to Muddear, Daddy, 11 of their then 12 children, but also where many cousins, other relatives and visiting friends laid their heads for many a night. The postage stamp-sized front and back yards gave the neighborhood playmates and me barely enough room to act out "Little Sally Walker" where four or more of us would join hands to sing and dance in a circle. Jumping rope, skipping on a stick drawn hopscotch of eight squares outlined in the dirt, jacks and marble shooting were the games of choice – one at a time – which we could fit in the small yard on Roosevelt Street.

As far as having limited space in our house on Roosevelt Street, Muddear and Daddy slept in one room, my brothers bunked in three sets of double bunk beds in another room and us girls slumbered in a smaller room that featured two sets of bunk beds, with two of the youngest of the then five girls sometimes sleeping two to a bed in one of the bottom beds.

The front room's decor included a full size sleeper sofa and a black and white 19-inch television fitted into a fake wooden console with rabbit ears pointing upward from its back. Oftentimes, we'd wake up to the end and coffee tables moved to the side of the front room and find ourselves stepping over pallets of cheap blankets and Grandmama's hand-sewn, heavy cotton padded, colorful quilts wrapped around several bodies of snoring cousins and friends of my brothers who frequently spent the night at our home.

Despite a small house crowded with lots of sleeping children, as morning came and Muddear stirred in the kitchen, aromas of grits, salmon patties, buttery biscuits, the fluffiest pancakes in the Delta and the worst coffee in the South permeated our home. Bodies awaken, yawned and stretched like lions getting ready for action, lining up in slow moves toward the tiny bathroom.

Moving to the Low End was going to be heaven. We would be living just a few miles South of downtown Cleveland and have two full bathrooms! Two full bathrooms would make days with a house full of folks trying to use one bathroom history. In fact, two bathrooms would even make my occasional nights spent at Grandmama's house seem like a blur.

To understand my bathroom issues and the appreciation of city services and other conveniences as they developed at the Haynes home and at Grandmama's house, I have to digress a little and take you on a short side story about Grandmama Estella. This insight often helps others appreciate why my siblings and I were hopeful about our move from uptown Cleveland to the Low End of town. My strict and very disciplined grandmother believed in saving the earth long before it was popular. She saved her old gum, chewing it and re-chewing it for days before she would discard it. Balls of chewed Doublemint or Spearmint gum were piled in a glass that set on the center of her kitchen table – ready to be plucked out for rechewing at Grandmama's passing by.

In fact, our paternal grandmother composted food as a habit. Egg shells, peelings from fruits and vegetables, the cobs left over from boiled corn, the hulls of peas shucked, old bread and spoiled leftover foods all went into her composts and later became feed for some of her yard animals or fertilizer for her gardens.

My Daddy's mother took frugality to a new height. Grandmama Estella's thriftiness started with her hard-earned income. Her money came from long days of laboring in cotton fields, selling her homemade peach and plum wines or the fresh vegetables and fruits from her backyard garden and the washing of laundry for families who lived across the tracks on the west side of town. That laundry of sheets, shirts and pants were often agitated by Grandmama's strong, large hands in a lye-based soapy water and scrubbed on wash boards, rinsed in clear water, hand-wrung of excess water and then hung to be sun-dried on her outdoor clothes line (Grandmama actually made the soap herself). The labor-intensive process ended after Grandmama used a heavy flatiron heated on her stovetop to press the linen and clothes to crisp perfection. She would then deliver the fresh laundry to the wives of the town's wealthy farmers and businessmen. For Grandmama, one dollar per basket of clothes was a banner day!

Those dollars – from laundry, food sales, working in the fields and from her husband's (our step grandfather whom we called Mr. Mack) income – never saw the inside of a bank account. After the 1927 market crash where she lost her life's savings at the time, Grandmama Estella just didn't trust banks. Instead of depositing her income, she carefully wrapped her money in waterproof bags and buried her savings in her back yard or inside her house, strategically placed in walls and floorboards. My eight year-old mind was told many times, "now baby, keep this a secret, but don't forget where your Grandmama is burying this." Of course, I forgot.

Grandmama Estella built her own home on Cross Street (just a block from East Side High School). She did it with her own hands, by herself! In my mind, she was a superwoman who believed that children should be seen and not heard!

While she had at least two bathrooms in her house, she didn't allow me to use them at night. Once we settled down for bed, if I had to use the toilet, I had to pull out the slop jar from under the bed. It didn't matter if I had to do number one (urinate) or do number two (make a bowel movement), the slop jar was the recipient of my waste for the night. After sitting on the slop jar, the rule was for me to wipe my private area, cover the jar and get back in bed. I would empty the slop jar the next morning. That saved on water, I guess, and kept us from tripping over stuff in her large but very overcrowded, overly furnished house.

Finally, Daddy had the house on the Low End ready enough, although not finished, for us to move in. On one of the days that we were moving things in, my brother Philip had been assigned by Daddy to work on the sewer. Something had gone wrong in the project and Philip had to dig about 10 feet deep through stinky, black, gunky cesspool sludge to fix the problem. It was the middle of July and the sun was beaming down on my brother's shirtless back as he sweated beads of frustration and anger. After all, he was stuck knee deep with doing one of the nastiest jobs at our new home. As I ran in and out of our new house, something came over me. I called out to Philip, pointing at him and chanting, "naw, naw, naw, naw, you smell like do-do." Philip pulled his six-foot, six-inch basketball-playing, pole-vaulting body out of the muddy, stinking sewer hole and headed my way as he swore that he was going to drop my barely into elementary school, four-foot body down the large polyurethane sewer tank. My brother looked like the creature from the black lagoon or a sewer monster who had risen from the bottom of the nearby Mississippi River. Mud and gunk were all over him and he was chasing me!

I ran and ran and ran with all my might – right smack dab into a tall pile of dirt that had been dug up to make way for our swimming pool. Sometime later, when I regained consciousness, my forehead was bleeding and my brother was holding me as he cried saying how sorry he was for scaring me. As I lay there weak and limp in his strong arms, the sewer stench engulfed my nostrils. I passed out again. My last waking thought was "the creature from the black lagoon caught me." The scar on my left eyebrow is a reminder of my blindly running from my brother – the creature, the sewer monster.

Little did we know that moving to the Low End would mean years of sewer problems. While our home was in the city limits, it and most of the others in the last few blocks of the Southern part of Cleveland were not privy to certain city services. From what I heard the elders say, getting tapped into the city's water line, having a blacktopped road, trucks regularly spraying for mosquitoes and police services were blessings to appreciate. After all, Mississippi Power & Light Company made sure our home and the Low End community had electricity.

The Delta Gas Company was fast digging lines to pipe gas for cooking and heating to homes in the community and replacing the large silver butane gas tanks that dotted the back yards of most of the Low End homes. The Haynes' abode was one of the first Low End houses to trade in the monster size butane tank for the low profile gas lines. It meant we also got rid of the large black stovepipe coal unit that stood in the middle of our family room!

Yet, the wait for sewer service would be long, tedious, political and frustrating, especially as the City of Cleveland opened a new 12-foot wide, eight-foot deep ditch to transfer open sewage from the west side of town to the sewer treatment lakes located on the other side of town. The horrible part was the uncovered ditch cut right through the Low End, and in many areas, was just a few feet from many of the homes on what is now called Glassco Street. Just weeks after the first flow of stench traveled the lengthy ditch to its resting place in the town's sewer processing lakes, the people in the community named the part that divided the Low End from the rest of Cleveland. Appropriately and respectful of the feelings of residents of the community, the open sewer became Cleveland's Grudge Ditch!

Not long after, when boarding Bolivar County Consolidated School District's bus number 23, I discovered that I was part of a gang. My siblings, the

Ramseys, the Randles, the Winters and all of us who waited together for the bus to take us to B. L. Bell Elementary School about five miles down the road in Boyle, Mississippi, were greeted by Mr. Friday who said, "I hope we got enough seats, cause here comes the Grudge Ditch Gang."

From then on, I realized everyone who lived south of the infamous Grudge Ditch was part of the Grudge Ditch Gang. We, in the Low End, had earned an identity by the gods of those who named kids who hung out together or lived in the same community as some kind of a gang. Similarly, those who lived in the alley behind downtown Cleveland were known by some as Alley Backs and by others as Alley Bats. Those who lived in the government supported public housing projects were known as the Project Rats. The kids from our neighborhood became the Grudge Ditch Gang. This name was given mainly because our parents had a grudge with the town leaders about running open sewage through our community and not providing our homes with public sewer services. Furthermore, we lived in the "Low End!"

Homebrew

Mr. DeBoy was no doubt six feet and four inches tall, that is, had he been able to stand. We kids always saw him awkwardly leaning and simultaneously somehow sitting his lanky body on a narrow four-legged wooden stool. His long immobile legs slanted across the porch's unpainted, weather-worn, pine planks to join the stool and porch for a perfect 90-degree triangle. Crisp dress pants and polished shoes were always part of his attire. I don't know how old he was or what physical thing had happened in his life that handicapped his ability to stand or walk without the aid of crutches. However, Mr. DeBoy ruled the world of the Grudge Ditch Gang when he was sitting two steps above ground out on his front porch. He saw and heard everything. While he could not get off his perch to come get us, all he had to do was call us in from whatever mischief we were in the midst of or about to get into and we had to acquiesce. Those of us who thought we could ignore him because he couldn't walk or run after us, soon found out it was best to answer his call. If he didn't use his fishing pole to reel us in like buffalo fish on a hook, he would send his sons out to catch us. The latter was the lesser desired of these two not preferred options. We all learned, one way or another, to just answer Mr. DeBoy's call.

One day, during the regular homebrew season, when people in the community gathered their ingredients to make their own special brand of beer or wine, I learned just how far of a reach Mr. DeBoy commanded. He and Mrs. Margie had 17 children. Their next-door neighbors, the Ramseys, had 10 children and a bunch of grandkids. Next door to them was Mr. Herman, who, to us kids was sort of a hermit, but he had a daughter (who was somewhere between my mother and my older sister's ages) and two grandchildren who were close to the ages of my youngest siblings. My family, who lived directly across the street from Mr. Herman, boasted 13 children. Next door to us were the famed Hurricane Club and its owners Mrs. Inez and Mr. JW. Surely wealthy, in our eyes, they had only two children, both adopted and who seemed to have everything the rest of us kids on the block hoped and dreamt our future would include. Mainly, our list included a brand new diamond in the back, luxury Lincoln Continental car with a sunroof top, Barbie dolls, the Hasbro Easy Bake Oven, bicycles, more toys, all the latest fashionable clothes and all the candy we could eat.

In addition to four night clubs, this little short block of 1800 Chrisman Avenue Extended had a few more families. The Randles lived behind Mr. DeBoy and Mrs. Margie. On the corner from Mr. Herman was the 400 Club and behind this nightclub was the home of the Winters' family. There were at least eight or nine children in their home. The rest of the land on that side of the block was a cemetery. On the other side of the block, next to my parents' few acres was Uncle Charles' junkyard of rusty, broken down cars and trucks that he harvested for his scrap metal and used auto parts business.

At the very end of South Chrisman Avenue Extended was the last of the nightclubs and certainly the most famous one –the Hole in the Wall. The likes of B.B. King, Bobbie Blue Bland, Son Thomas and other famous blues singers made regular appearances early in their careers at the Hole in the Wall. Several of my siblings and I earned our pocket change as preteens cleaning up the Hole in the Wall. On Saturday mornings and other mornings throughout the summers, we would arrive early at the night club to collect beer bottles and remove discarded dirty thin paper plates and even thinner napkins soiled with drippings from barbecued rib tips or crispy fried chicken wings or finger-licking-good pork chops. We literally washed the floors that smelled like beer and urine with buckets of Pine Sol infused water – scrubbing the rough wood and slick linoleum areas with a broom and then a mop that was bigger than most of us. Shortly after getting paid for our work, the quarters earned by each of us were hurriedly taken to Mrs. Margie's store for frozen Popsicles or other treats. We also picked up trash from our own lawn. The trash was not ours, but trash discarded on our lawn by patrons of the neighboring Hurricane Club. We tried to charge Mr. J.W. and Mrs. Inez for our labor, but Daddy found out and made us give the hard earned dollars back to the Fosters. We also tried charging patrons a dollar each for parking on our property. Daddy discovered this enterprise, too, and threatened to tan our hides if we even thought about charging the people who tore up and trashed our property just so they could patronize the Hurricane Club. However, we did salvage many of the discarded bottles from the nightclub patrons. Mr. DeBoy would sterilize the bottles and re-use them for bottling his homebrew.

Mr. DeBoy's homebrew often complimented the Schlitz malt liquor, Jax, Falstaff and Miller Highlife beers at the Hole in the Wall, the 400 Club, the Hurricane Club and even his wife Mrs. Margie's unlicensed big cooler in the back of her two-room wood-framed store (one of the rooms at Mrs. Margie's business was also a sort of club hangout).

It was late summer, after the cotton-chopping season and right before the cotton-picking season in the Mississippi Delta. This sort of a break meant that many of the older children in the community were home, not in the fields working to earn five or ten dollars a day to help their families make ends meet or to help buy themselves school clothes or a pair of white, red-trimmed All Star Converse tennis shoes.

For us Haynes kids, that meant we didn't have to sneak off to the cotton fields just so we could hang out with our friends, thus defying our dad's proclamation that "his children better not ever, as long as we were black and our butts turned to the ground, never, ever be caught on a bus or pickup truck going to the cotton fields." Well, for us, that meant forever. So we sneaked off to the cotton fields. I guess with so many kids, no telephone and our playing range spreading as much as a mile from one house to another, it was probably hard for our mother to know when two or three of us went missing for several hours. The cardinal rule in our world was to get home before dark and make sure Muddear knew where we were going. So telling her where our initial stop was didn't mean she needed to know all our subsequent stops, we decided.

Daddy was trying to protect us from some of the dangers of working in the cotton fields, such as being sprayed with the deadly DDT (Dichloro-diphenyltricholoroethane) that misted from small airplanes flying low across the cotton fields and sometimes across our homes. DDT was banned in many countries across the globe and in several cotton producing states in America, despite protests by many farmers that the pesticide was a low-cost and effective way to rid cotton fields of deadly pests. The Mississippi farmers prevailed for many years until the federal government outlawed use of the chemical. The farmers were especially concerned about the notorious boll weevil that threatened to wipe out cotton plantations and farms all over the Mississippi Delta. In the meantime, residents of the Mississippi Delta just suffered the potential dangers for many more years. Years later, after being removed from the market, DDT was considered by many as the source of so much of the cancer that disproportionately attacked many Mississippi Delta residents.

I suspect Daddy's bigger mission was to keep his children as far away as possible from the remnants of sharecropping and slavery. Chopping and picking cotton were too close for comfort for Daddy. His father, L.D. Haynes, Sr., occasionally sharecropped between disagreements with his boss at the local Solomon Delivery Service Company. Most of us Haynes children never met Grandpa Haynes. He died or disappeared before half of us were born. We were told that he couldn't read or write, but he found his way around Cleveland and Bolivar County on behalf of Solomon. Making deliveries via mules pulling wagon loads of goods that ranged from foods to lumber supplies, Grandpa Haynes was the only person I ever heard of who worked harder than my Daddy and my Grandmother Estella. In a blast from the past files, the Cleveland *Bolivar Commercial Newspaper* ran a photo of Grandpa Haynes in front of the first motorized vehicle to arrive in Cleveland. The vehicle was purchased by Grandpa Haynes' employer, the Solomon Company, to improve delivery times. With the first motorized vehicle, Grandpa Haynes had an increased workload without an increase in pay or help. In protest, occasionally he would quit his job rather than be unfairly used by the Solomon Company owners. In those times, he would find himself back on the farm, sharecropping and committing himself, Grandmama, Uncle Robert and Daddy to bringing in bales and bales of cotton.

Those times made Daddy sign up for the Army as soon as he was of age. His brother Robert left home at the age of 16, traveling all the way to Los Angeles, California, where he made his life until he died just a few years ago. Uncle Robert never graced the State of Mississippi with his presence again after he crossed the state line heading west. As far as Daddy's story goes, he married my mother when he was 19 and she was 14. He got out of sharecropping and into the U.S. Army where he also got to see the world, fighting in both the Korean War and World War II. Thanks to the life he and his parents and brother experienced sharecropping, Daddy decided he would rather fight for his country than sharecrop. Sharecropping was never going to be his way to make a living.

While he was the king maker of children working hard, he wanted his children to have no part of labor that reminded him of sharecropping and slavery. Furthermore, he no doubt thought that our few acres of farm animals and gardens offered plenty of work to keep all 13 of his children productive without going off to cotton fields where several children had lost their lives.

Daddy put his foot down most firmly on the issue of any of us going to the fields after my brothers Terry and Philip joined several of Mrs. Margie's sons in a summer trek to the tobacco fields of North Carolina. They called themselves running away from home with dreams of making it big by picking tobacco leaves and staying at a farm dormitory. They were barely 16 or so, but stole away in the late hours of the night while Daddy was working out of town. Eight weeks after they left, like prodigal sons, the barefooted, hungry, physically tattered and financially depleted Terry, Philip and several other Grudge Ditch older boys stole their way back to the Low End. Their "run-away-child" stories were regaled in the Temptations' number one hit song that touted "...you better go back home, where you belong..."

Even after Daddy placed my brothers Philip and Terry on punishment for several months, they didn't mind

Daddy's strictness. They were so happy to be back home with Muddear's home cooking, a warm bed, a roof over their head, in-door plumbing, warm bath water, clean clothes and a loving family. While they didn't talk about their tobacco field days much, some 40 years later, Terry shared painful details about having to eat from garbage cans and literally having no shoes as he and his friends walked miles to try to get back home. For sure, my older brothers never wanted to see themselves as laborers in a cotton field, let alone a tobacco field, again!

Cotton season or not, the children of every family had many chores to finish before being free to play. If one group finished their chores first, that group usually visited neighbors and helped those children to finish their chores so that we could all play together. Oftentimes, we'd try to sneak in playtime amidst our chores. The chores ran the gamut, but generally focused on getting food on the table. Chopping or pulling weeds from each family's huge acre or two of rows of garden vegetables was a given. Then, depending on the season, we could be found picking corn, greens, beans, tomatoes, cucumbers, cantaloupes, watermelons, okra and sweet potatoes and harvesting other staples to help our parents in feeding our large families. Feeding the scattering of chickens, carrying buckets of hog "slop" to the pig pen for the hogs and their pigs, mowing the lawn and planting seeds were just a few of our many, many chores around the home.

Always, helping our parents in their various enterprises was par for the course. Hide-and-seek, dancing, racing and imitating the Temptations, James Brown, the Pips, the Supremes, Richard Pryor and other stars also infiltrated our work ethics.

Surely, in one stage or another of Mr. DeBoy's two-month home brewing session, all hands – whether they were of a five-year-old or an 18-year-old – were useful. Long before microbreweries were the cool, hip thing to do, Mr. DeBoy was sorting out hops, fermenting his brew and bottling it for his select friends and clientele. And the children of the Low End, inherent members of the Grudge Ditch Gang, were learning one more useful trade. (Were we bootleggers, too, since it wasn't until the late 1970s that President Jimmy Carter legalized home breweries?) When our neighborhood beer guru started gathering his ingredients, the children in our block knew our play time would severely diminish due to the homebrew chores Mr. DeBoy had scheduled for his kids. The rest of us might as well line up to help if we were ever going to play stick ball, dodge ball, basketball, wrestle, create our own baby dolls of corn hair and discarded soda bottles or just run freely up and down the neighborhood.

Mr. DeBoy's favorite child, Florida, was close in age to me, eight years old, and one of my best friends. As Mr. DeBoy was calling us to strain hop or malt balls or seeds of stuff from the foamy, yeasty smelling batch of beer-in-the-making, Florida was taunting and challenging me into a wrestling match. Since my little sisters, Phyllis, Toni, Rena and San were watching and her sisters Yvonne and Boodie wanted to see who was the toughest, we ran right past Mr. DeBoy like fighting roosters. Florida pushed me hard and dared me to fight her back. Like a bull seeing red, I did a back peddling with my right foot in the dusty soil and dove toward Florida with every intention of knocking her out with my best Jim Brown NFL tackle. As I came within a few inches of her, she adeptly stepped aside and every part of my body, especially my head and face that were looking to tackle Florida made a full imprint into the ground just behind where Florida once stood. The rest of my body and my embarrassed, deflated ego also fell to the ground. When I came up for air, my dirt-dusted face, matted with tears of anger, had me looking like a mad fool. Undaunted, I prepared again to mow down my friend who was at that moment, enemy number one.

As I dug in my heels and prepared to charge again, the tip of what I believed was the world's longest fishing pole tapped Florida on her legs. "Yawl come here. Didn't you hear me calling you? Get over here, now," said the stern voice of Florida's daddy. As he preached to us, we both felt like fish that didn't get away. The whipping with the fishing pole must be what fish feel as they are being scaled alive. Cry? No way. With Mr. DeBoy, the more you cried, the more you were whipped. Unlike with my daddy, the more we cried, the fewer licks we got from his belt. "Now go wash your hands and get back here to help me with this homebrew," Mr. DeBoy commanded as all of my younger sisters and Florida's younger sisters magically disappeared. I surmised that they didn't want to risk being within reach of Mr. DeBoy's wrath or fishing pole, and they certainly didn't want to get locked into making beer.

The making of beer didn't seem as dangerous as wine-making, but our younger sisters were fearful of the process. Their classmates had shared stories about Melvin and Milton Latham from Boyle. The two brothers had practically blown up their family's barn because they were making wine without their father's knowledge. They forgot to let their fermenting peach wine "breathe." Consequently, after a few days, several large jugs of fermenting peach wine overheated and blew up! The small barn was destroyed. Thinking about that fiasco reaffirmed in my mind that I would help Florida out in the making of beer as long as it was on their front porch. For sure, I wasn't going anywhere near the sealed tight containers of homebrew in Mr. DeBoy's cool, dark storage room. If I had to do that, our friendship would end because I would do like my sisters, run on back across the street to our house where Daddy brought home plenty of beer already made, factory sealed in cans and bottles. In fact, according to my sisters Toni and Phyllis, they liked Daddy's iced cold frosty factory-produced beer a lot better than they liked Mr. DeBoy's hot smelly homebrew.

Since I was so dusty from being faked out by my friend, I went to the outdoor pump in the Carters' back yard, primed it with a cup of water, and reveled in the cool flow that washed my hands, face and arms and then whetted my thirst. I gave the pump a few more pushes on its iron handle and Florida washed her hands and cupped them for a drink of the sweetest, softest water we had ever tasted. We rushed back to the front porch, hand in hand, once again good friends, where Mr. DeBoy proceeded to direct us in the fine art of brewing beer.

The Grave Yard

Years later, as I visit home, I have to smile at how the turn of events developed the Low End. Some time after the hip 400 Club went out of business, Uncle Charles and Aunt Mamie got a divorce. Uncle Charles built himself a small house on the lot where the club once stood on the corner of the now Winnie Street and South Chrisman Avenue Extended. The latter street always had been named so, but I don't remember how or when the graveyard street that ran perpendicular to Chrisman Avenue earned my mother's name.

Uncle Charles was not brother to my mom or dad, but he and my dad were close friends and consequently, like aunts and uncles to each other's children.

Uncle Charles' house bordered the graveyard lot.Mr. Herman's shotgun house was also wrapped in the asbestos black and gray tar-based shingles. It, too, bordered the graveyard and faced our house on Chrisman Avenue. The Winters' green Jim Walter pre-fabricated house faced the then unnamed graveled road, now paved and called Winnie Street. Between the back of the Winters' house and the side of Mr. Herman's home, as well as several blocks to the west, were graves, upon graves, upon graves that blended to an endless horizon. The cemetery seemed like a black hole of darkness on the west side with every night fall.

One Saturday morning, I heard my older brothers and some of the older neighborhood guys laying out a plan to teach a lesson to the notoriously handsome but doggishly evil Walter Johnson. Many of the older girls thought Walter was cool because he had a car – a fancy candy apple red Buick at that. However, word had gotten around how Mr. Big Stuff would entice a date into his car, promising her a convenient ride home. His modus operandi was always to take a short cut through the graveyard where he would park his car, tell the unsuspecting girl that if she didn't give him what he wanted, she would have to walk home. If the girl even made an attempt to get out of the car, he would proceed to force himself upon the unwitting victim. The Grudge Ditch Gang of older boys didn't like Walter's tactics and many of them were probably jealous of his car and fancy clothes. They had heard about his plans for a new girl in town whom he was taking to the Saturday night dance. The dance was being held at the community center located in mid-town on the corners of Chrisman Avenue and Murphy Street. The gang left the dance early, donned an array of carefully designed costumes and headed to their pre-selected hiding spots in the graveyard.

Right on time, Walter pulled up and parked between two headstones. His larger than life, delicious red deuce and a quarter, officially known as the Buick Electra 225, was so out of place. The car's white leather seats were trimmed in white fur that seemed to cradle and nearly suffocate Walter and his date. When Walter's guest didn't succumb to his oily words, Walter started to get physical with her. As the pair of four-inch red and white dice swung about the car's rear view mirror, Walter heard a ghostly "boooooo" outside his car window. Slowing his unwelcomed advances on his date, Walter saw something appear in front of his car. An eerie, fanged-toothed, white-faced, bloody-looking 12-foot figure rose up from the dark shadows of the graveyard. At the car's rear bumper, the rear end of the car was being lifted up and down. On the passenger's side of the car, there were loud thumps.

My brothers, Terry, Philip, Lester and Sammy, (joined by our cousins Fehl and Kirk and their friends

Mookie, Toadie, J.V., Tank and Bobby), could hardly contain themselves from laughter as a spooked Walter, frightened out of his wits, abandoned his date. He leaped from his car and took off running faster than lightening past grave markers, plastic flowers, stone crosses, little American flags and momentarily into an open grave that was being dug for a Monday burial. Walter bounced up out of the open grave, screaming something unintelligible and continued to sprint out on to Winnie Street, past Chrisman Avenue and through Uncle Charles' junkyard on toward U.S. Highway 61.

The new girl in town was quite grateful and that was the last time Walter Johnson bragged about how he got his girls. My brothers, cousins and the older members of the Grudge Ditch Gang laughed themselves silly that Saturday night as they pulled hanging moss from their arms and washed the bloody looking Heinz catsup and ghostly white shoe polish off themselves. Their laughter continued for many weeks afterward as they re-enacted how a black-caped Bobby stood on Sammy's shoulders to look giant size tall as they scared the bejeezus out of Walter.

Milk Rash & Incredible Hulk

I awakened in the middle of the night to find my hands were still tied behind my back. They had white cotton socks on them, too. My face was itching so bad that I wanted to tear off my skin. I twisted and turned but couldn't get my hands loose, so I decided to just rub my face against the ridges of the brown paneled wall next to the bottom level bunk bed where I laid. As I felt blood running down my cheeks, I knew I had gone too far. This milk rash was surely going to be the death of me. When it wasn't making me scar my cheeks, it was attacking the tender areas in the fold of my elbows or behind my knees.

No wonder some of the kids in school found themselves snickering, pointing at and calling me the Incredible Hulk. The Marvel Comics hero featured Dr. David Banner who, when angered, transformed into a creature with green unappealing skin. Although my condition of skin rash didn't occur because of some gamma ray experiment gone bad, even as a child, I felt that something was going on in the Delta air that always had my skin inflamed. The "milk rash" had me scratching my skin to points of no return.

Many children in the neighborhood grew up drinking some formula of milk from the Sunflower or the Piggly Wiggly grocery stores. However, most of the mothers in the Low End served up a mixture of the commodity milk handed out to families living below the poverty level. For our cereal bowls and our siblings' bottles, powdered milk mixed with water tasted as good as the cow or goat's milk. Living below the poverty level qualification meant all of the Low End families waited with much anticipation for the powdered milk.

Grandmama Estella often laughed with Muddear, saying she would "rather clothe than feed" us, especially my athletic brothers who would eat any food put in front of them. They often supplemented the meals Muddear cooked with snacks from the various pear and plum trees in our back yard or raw sweet potatoes, cucumbers, cantaloupes, strawberries or watermelons pulled straight from the vines in our garden. A favorite snack for us all was from the commodity foods found on Muddear's kitchen shelves. Raisins from large white boxes were the reach in, grab and go snack. Peanut butter from large white cans were spread on thin slices of Wonder bread for a quick sandwich.

The proud L.D. Haynes would not allow Muddear or any of his children to stand in line for government assistance. He just didn't believe in his family receiving handouts or aid. However, his mother had a different view. She told Muddear, "What L.D. doesn't know won't hurt him and the commodity food I bring you will help feed these growing children!" So Grandmama stood in the cheese line and every commodity food line that came to Cleveland. When Daddy was out of town on one of his road trips, she would bring bags and boxes of cheese, peanut butter, powdered milk and more to our house on Chrisman Avenue Extended. Furthermore, Muddear complemented Grandmama's provisions of commodity groceries with her own collection of foods brought to her by many of her clients – those who wanted her to bake a cake or press and curl their hair. They traded and bartered with supplies when money was low. Yes, money was low almost all the time.

We were especially ecstatic about the big chunks of cheese, bags of rice, and large white generic cans of meat that simply read in bold black Times Roman font – 'USDA Approved Beef,' 'USDA Approved Pork' or 'USDA Approved Chicken.' However, for Mrs. Winnie's middle child, me, that is, goat's milk was the only milk that would not break me out in blotches of what Muddear and Daddy referred to as "milk rash." Decades later, I learned that my "milk rash" is medically referred to as atopic dermatitis and eczema.

Somehow, my parents, my hard-working, baby-making machines Muddear and Daddy, found a way around the poverty in which most of us kids didn't even realize we lived. When I was too old for my mother's breast milk, the expensive goat milk was mine to have in cereal or just as a cold glass of it to drink as a morning refreshment. (Now that I reflect on those days, I wonder if my milk came from the goat that Mr. Herman had fenced in his yard directly across the street from our house. Most of the kids in the neighborhood assumed Mr. Herman got the goat because he hated mowing grass. The goat nibbled Mr. Herman's grass low to the ground so he didn't have to mow his lawn at all. Just imagine, Mr. Herman's goat was probably my milk benefactor.

On the morning that my sister Florida Rena ran to tell Muddear that I was bleeding all over the place from rubbing my itchy face on the bedroom wall's brown, particle-pressed, simulated wooden paneling, Muddear gathered me in her arms. She loosened the restraints on my hands and cried with me as she applied cold wet towel compresses to my abused face. When Dr. Searcy came by with Aunt Chicken (Uncle Louie's wife, who was of no blood relation either, but Daddy's business partner at the service station), I quickly realized this was one time I would not be able to get away from my biggest fear at this point in my life – needles!

A nurse by profession, Aunt Chicken pulled a little white-labeled clear bottle out of her black medical bag. Dr. Searcy told her to make it so many CCs – more than what she normally came out to give me once a week. It seemed like slow motion as Aunt Chicken drew what appeared to me as the world's longest needle from her bag. She uncapped the end that covered the needle's sharp point, held the small bottle up toward the ceiling, punctured its rubbery top with the needle and withdrew the steroidal medicine into the syringe. Dr. Searcy, the kindest doctor – the only doctor I knew – firmed his grip on me as Muddear turned me over enough to pull my panties down to expose the upper cheek of my rump. I screamed, tried to kick and went into all kinds of conniptions when I saw the needle coming toward my body. With one hand, Aunt Chicken swabbed a spot on my gluteus maximus with an alcohol drenched cotton ball and said, "Shush, honey, it's not going to hurt, it will be just like a little pinch." She lied. As she deftly used her other hand to punch my behind with the needle, I screamed and blacked out to a foggy state somewhere between barely awake and endless sleep. I heard Dr. Searcy remind my mother – you can't let her scratch her face, she will be marred for life. Babies born with this usually grow out of it. Be patient, Jessie will grow out of it, too.

Nearly 50 years later, I have not grown out of eczema. As troublesome, I am still fearful of needles and have often passed out as technicians and nurses try to stick me to draw my blood. Like my Daddy passed it on to me, I seem to have passed on a milder version of eczema and atopic dermatitis to my daughters and granddaughter.

Dirty Diapers

Although we had a laundry room inside our Low End home, Daddy had yet to get around to finishing the room for its designed purpose. There was something tricky about having enough electrical power to run the one cycle Speen Clean Wringer Washer. It used more power than most appliances, despite requiring several manual functions. We had to feed clothes through its rollers to squeeze excess water from them after they were washed. Although there was no government water rationing policy, Muddear and Daddy made sure that we conserved water and electricity. All the clothes were washed in the same load of water. Sorting the lightest and least soiled items from the dark and/or heaviest soiled laundry started each laundry day. Washing for as many as 15-20 people (including the often visiting relatives) meant laundry days at least two or three times a week.

For the whites, we started the load of water with bleach, a cup or two of Tide Laundry Detergent and a square of bluing to make the whites whiter and the colors brighter. While it seemed like weird science to my sisters and me, the bluing that sometimes smeared our fingers when we mishandled it, actually did make the white linen wash whiter, despite turning our pale fingers a deep navy blue. After the whites were washed, we made small pastes of the Tide and Purex bleach to try to wash the bluing off our hands. Too bad our parents didn't own stock in Tide, the Haynes family used several large boxes of the detergent every month.

The Speen Clean agitated the dirt from the clothes and linen. Load by load, the water became darker and darker. Once all the loads were washed, first the whites, then the light colors and finally the dark items, the sudsy water was drained from the four-legged tub that had a motorized blue agitator at its center. The agitator swished back and forth to shake the dirt and grime from our laundry. Mind you, there was no spin cycle – just a wash cycle. The whole cycle had to be repeated for rinsing the clothes in clear cold water. After squeezing them through the wringer again, we would take the clothes to be hung and secured with wooden clothespins to the long wire clothesline at the back of our house. Muddear was a firm believer that whatever dirt was missed in the wash cycle would be eliminated in the rinse cycle. Hence, the old adage of "if the wash doesn't get it, the rinse will" was popular among the mothers in our neighborhood.

Once the clothes were clean with soapy water and agitation, the roller unit that sat on the top edge of the washer was flipped in to action. One by one, my sisters and I, depending on whose turn it was, fed shirts, pants, underwear, socks, diapers, sheets, towels, dresses and other items through the roller wringer arms of the Speen Clean Wringer Washer. This tedious process meant we had to be focused because that roller wringer sometimes got greedy and would suck our hands and arms between its rollers. For sure, I thought one day that greedy machine was going to go crazy and roll not just our hands through its wringer, but flatten each of us and pull our entire bodies through its rollers.

The Speen Clean Wringer Washer was finally moved to the outside of the house to avoid the potential major issue of water backing up into the house. Despite Daddy's best efforts, he was unsuccessful in connecting the drain pipe from the washing machine to the sewer line leading to the 16-foot- deep cesspool (that was a sort of in-ground covered septic tank) located just a few yards from our back door. Finally, a frustrated Muddear had my brothers to move the four-legged monster of a machine outside to a covered area where we hung out to cool off from the stifling heat that the fans in our house just seem to stir and make hotter. Room had to be made for the washing machine at the edge of this wooden roofed, dirt floored, unfinished patio that was host to children and adults alike for 'shooting the bull' or 'trash talking' and playing checkers, dominoes and card games of spades, gin rummy, tonk and even old maid, depending on the age group or skill level.

Muddear had given birth to her 13th and last child, Sandra. Despite, her quiet, easy and go-along-to-get-along nature, hand washing diapers, breast feeding a hungry child, cooking for 12 other children and cleaning house were finally more than Muddear's own house laws allowed. So outside went the washing machine and much to the chagrin of my older sister Malinda, any of the cool kids visiting or passing by would now get to see her washing clothes at least two days a week! "Where was the justice," she murmured? After all, she had already been seen with her mouth stuffed with clothespins as she manipulated the hanging of diapers on our clothesline that had to be longer than the one at Mr. Ben's Laundry & Dry Cleaning Services.

The most tedious part of the laundry was washing the diapers of our new baby sister Sandra. The ones soiled with just urine were easy. It was those stinking "do-do" diapers that often made my church-singing sister Malinda lay down her religion so she could take care of business the way the devil wanted her to. Since Phyllis, Rena, Toni and I were not quite skilled at getting the diapers really sanitized, our older sister Malinda was most often assigned this chore by Muddear. I was in training to help Malinda out. The next sister in line was Phyllis. She had already gotten out of washing clothes for a couple of weeks by getting her hand and half of her arm caught in the wringer arms of the washing machine. That gave her a temporary bye from diaper-washing duty.

For whatever reason – whatever Muddear was feeding San – probably a mashed version of turnip greens picked fresh from our garden, San had a banner day of bowel movements. As such, Malinda and I as her assistant got a banner day of washing soiled, dookie diapers. With a bucket of water on the ground, each soiled diaper had to be first rinsed and assured no boo-boo was left on them before going into the washing machine. Malinda was having a difficult time with the smell, when Bobby walked by and began teasing her – shouting, "Hey wash woman, you got do-do all over you."

My sister, who was truly the mouth of the South, shouted back, "your mama got do-do all over her." The dozens were on. Bobby and Malinda traded insults until Malinda got so mad that she gathered one of San's nastiest diapers – saturated with yellow and green poop – in the hand of her baseball pitching arm and aimed it for Bobby's head. As he saw the missile hurling his way, Bobby took off running toward his home across the street. However, his reaction was a second too late. Malinda's diaper bombshell was a homerun as it exploded on Bobby's back and she sealed the deal with "Now run and tell that to your mama!"

Yep, I hated washing dirty diapers and disposable Pampers could not come too soon. Yet, at that moment, my sister was the queen of the Low End. I was proud to stand at her side as the chief assistant do-do diaper washer.

Trash House

Living in the country as opposed to town changed our lives in a number of ways. Most ways were greatly positive to us young kids because we had lots of breathing room and plenty of space to run around and play. I found a hide away in the nearby woods where vines and foliage covered a smooth, earthen dusty dirt flooring. The area was perfect for playing house, jacks, marbles and just getting away from the bustling activities of the real world in the Haynes household. Some of my quietest childhood moments were spent gently rocking on a homemade hammock of a worn sheet stretched between two trees. Oftentimes joined by friends, we were cooled from the steamy hot Delta days with breezes and the shelter of a rich abundance of green kudzu leaves above our heads. The Haynes home was located about a half mile away from my private hideaway. Until nightfall, peace and quiet were commodities hard to come by in a house full of siblings who all seemed to have our Daddy's gift of gab.

Just as freedom to roam in a wider range from home was a positive factor about living in the Low End, the negatives included inconveniences such as not being connected to a fully working sewer sanitation system and not having twice a week curbside trash pickup by the city's garbage collection trucks and crew. Although we had an address of South Chrisman Avenue Extended, Cleveland, MS 38732 – the same zip code that we had when we lived in town on Roosevelt Street, we did not have the city services because our homes were located in the recently annexed Low End of Cleveland. Consequently, whatever services Bolivar County or the City of Cleveland didn't offer, my Daddy had to provide himself or have a private contractor do the services. The Low End fathers worked hard to provide their own waste management and water services (well water for cooking, drinking, bathing and cleaning). This included digging their own cesspool or installing in-ground sanitation septic tank systems for sewage disposal. Burning their own trash was also among the self-provided services the Low End residents found themselves working into their way of life. Whether the now removed city families as the Randles who were former "Alley Backs" or "Alley Bats" from the downtown Cleveland area or the newly relocated Ramseys who moved to the Low End from the deep woods (the real country that was Southeast of Boyle), every household had to learn how to manage their waste. ("Alley Backs" and "Alley Bats" were names similar to the Grudge Ditch Gang –given to those who lived in downtown Cleveland, beyond the main streets and beyond the alleys behind the main streets on to the small, narrow dirt and occasionally graveled lanes behind the alleys. These back alleys were bordered with too many and too close, small shotgun, wood-framed, whitewashed row houses and shacks. The residents, especially the children of this community were called "Alley Bats" by most and "Alley Backs" by others. One thing we all believed, if we ever had to be in a fight, we did not want it to be against the Alley Bats because we feared many of them would just as soon shoot, slice or stab their enemies at the slightest provocation.)

One particular week, not too long after the harsh persistent winds of a low-grade tornado had stirred up the entire Mississippi Delta, Daddy decided he would build a simple framed area to house our trash until the monthly trash-burning days came around. That way, the next time a strong wind blew through town, the Haynes' family trash would not be strewn all over the Delta. The first day, my brothers dug several narrow deep holes, each about five feet apart, covering the square area of about 20 feet by 20 feet. On the second day, Daddy showed them how to mix concrete, pour it in the holes and set the heavy, oily black, thick and tall discarded railroad crossties in the concrete filled holes. On the third day, my older brothers started nailing the horizontal sheets of wavy silver tin to the poles. With most of the work done, except for the vertical door cover and the painting, my older brothers went on a quick turn around road trip with Daddy to pick up an emergency load of Schlitz and Old Milwaukee beers. Daddy gave clear instructions to my youngest brother Randy on how to finish the construction job, including fitting the door to a vertical sheet of the shiny tin. He further instructed Randy to allow me to help paint the project once all the hammering and nailing were done.

I was so excited that Daddy trusted me with such an important job. Randy and I finished the mustard yellow painting of the tin and stood back to look at our work. We were proud and ran to call Muddear to look at what we'd done. She gave us kudos and told us how proud Daddy was going to be to see the beautiful yellow facility that would now secure the family's trash.

Later that day, I was bored and feeling proud about the trash house's painting project. I got this very bright and genius idea that I thought would help everyone in our home recognize the unique purpose of the trash house. Furthermore, I thought this finishing touch would make Daddy even prouder of the work Randy and I did. Digging through Daddy's workshop, I found a small can of brown paint – a perfect match for the mustard yellow color already adorning the tin trash pen. In three-foot letters, big enough to be seen about a half acre away from U.S. Highway 61 that bordered our property on the east, I painted the letters T-R-A-S-H on one line. On the second line, in letters that would garner an "E" for excellent from my third grade teacher Mrs. Bibbs, I stroked out the letters H-O-U-S-E. I stood back, admiring my work which was really my first "billboard." Feeling like God must have felt on the day he looked out over the universe and made the stars, I said to myself – "trash house – now that's good. No one will mistake this for the house we live in since I have clearly displayed its name 'trash house' where all can see it. Daddy will be so proud."

Just as the sun was setting over the west side of town, I heard Daddy blow the horn of his beer-laden transport truck. I looked out toward U.S. Highway 61 and waved as Daddy honked his horn again and headed a few more miles north on the highway to dock the truck for unloading at the Wells' warehouse. It wouldn't be long before Daddy would arrive home to see my contribution to the trash house. Yes, he's going to love it, I thought.

Muddear started her homecoming ritual for Daddy, preparing his meal and getting his bath ready. Since Daddy and the Fosters, who were our next door neighbors South of our property, had dug deep to strike well water on our adjoining land, Daddy and all of us in the Haynes household relished in bathing in this soft well water. Muddear had made it her married lifelong habit of joy to have hot bath water waiting on Daddy whenever he returned from a road trip. Her signal that he would be home within the hour was a special series of horn honks Daddy's truck made as he passed by our house on the highway adjacent to our property. A hot home-cooked meal was also part of what greeted Daddy when he stepped inside the door at at our home on South Chrisman Avenue Extended. Of course, a loving wife and many, many rambunctious children who were happy to jump around his neck, hang on his back or pull on his legs were part of our standard expressions of happiness about Daddy's homecoming ritual. (That is, we were that way when Daddy arrived home during normal hours. When he arrived in the wee hours of the night while we were all asleep, Daddy would be the rambunctious one. He'd come in and tickle us awake or blast the house with sounds of rhythm and blues as "Lucille," "Frankie & Johnnie" or "Polk Salad Annie." When we would sleepily acknowledge that Daddy was home, the house would again be quiet as Muddear served him his breakfast.

Frankly, because he drove thousands of miles each week, the odds were high that he would be involved in an accident that would hamper his coming home to us. The Haynes children will always remember the time that Daddy's truck flipped over repeatedly from atop an Appalachian mountain in Tennessee. Beer flew everywhere. After the truck came to a rest at the foot of the mountain, Daddy's truck was pried and cut open with the Jaws of Life to remove him from the smashed metal. Still alive, the only damage done was to his ego for marring his accident-free record and to his little finger that was broken. The state trooper told Daddy that travelers passing by had taken most of the beer that was on or near the truck. He went on to explain to Daddy that it was truly a miracle for him to have survived the accident. "God must have left you alive for a reason," the state trooper said. Daddy quipped, "Yes, those people who passed by and thought I was dead must have needed that beer. That's why they took it. My wife and 13 children need me, and that's why God left me here and let me live."

Daddy arrived home too late to see Randy's and my trash house handiwork. It was too dark, since night fell early that day. I had fallen asleep, weary from all my hard labor. Daddy, too, must have been weary from the long drive and then the unloading of a few hundred cases of beer from the 18-wheeler transport truck to the several smaller local distribution trucks. I was awakened the next morning, bright and early by a stern-faced Daddy who was holding the dreaded belt in his hand. "Get up Jessie. I want you to tell me what was on your mind when you decided to embarrass the whole family by painting 'trash house' in larger than life letters on the trash house"? He was really mad and I was in disbelief as he told me to lie across the chair for my whipping. "Whoop," "whoop" and "whoop" were heard as Daddy's belt met my behind. I screamed from the sting as though my Daddy was killing me. In a sense, he was. He was killing my spirit to be creative, to take risks or to dare to be or do things different. "The next time you decide you want to deface someone's property, you had better ask first, you understand," he stated instead of allowing me to answer. "Yes sir Daddy," I cried, still in a state of disbelief and confusion. "Now get dressed, you have a paint job to do. When I come home this evening, I don't want to see any writing on the trash house, just yellow paint," he said quietly as he walked away from my whimpering, sniffling cries.

Randy heard me getting my whipping and correctly surmised that he had one coming, too. I guess Daddy decided Randy should have had the sense to discourage me from identifying the trash house in big bold letters. Randy hid out the entire day and Daddy waited him out. Everyone knew Randy loved to eat. There was no doubt that he would come home in time for dinner. Plus, he would get into more trouble if night fell and he was not in the house.

When a hungry Randy finally came home, Daddy was there with his belt. I didn't hear the discussion Daddy had with Randy, but I heard the tousling as Randy tried to get away from Daddy and the pain-rendering belt. I had taken my whipping like a girl, consequently, I received three licks and it was over. Randy was trying to run from and struggle with Daddy like a man-child. Daddy wore Randy out and Randy wore Daddy out. His whipping seemed to last forever. Then, Randy ate his dinner and went to bed.

Later that night, when I got up to go to the bathroom, I heard Muddear and Daddy talking. Daddy said, "These kids are getting too big for me to whip them. I think I threw my back out trying to whip some sense into Randy. We have to find another way to help them know right and to do right." I eased back to the girls' bedroom, got on my knees and said, "Thank you, Jesus!"

Road Runner

The railroad track was just southwest of the Low End. It crossed a big drainage ditch that bordered the very last street in Cleveland. Just about a half block behind the world renowned Hole in the Wall nightclub located at the very end of South Chrisman Avenue Extended was a link of the Illinois Central Railroad. This track is about 30 miles southeast of the famous one called "Where the Southern crosses the Yellow Dog" rails. That's Indianola, home of the king of the blues, Mr. B.B. King. (As famous then for stories of his flirtations as he was and still is known today for the blues, the king reportedly dated my Aunt Pluke for a short stint. When I interviewed him years later as a news reporter for the *Delta Democrat-Times Newspaper* in Greenville, Mr. King shared fond memories of performing at the Hole in the Wall. However, he had no memory of my Aunt Pluke.)

Facing the Hole in the Wall was Mr. Stoney's place. It covered a narrow strip of land that stretched from U.S. Highway 61 to South Chrisman Avenue Extended and was blanketed with tall blades of hay. To us children, it was just tall wild grass that needed to be cut down with one of Daddy's sling blades. We later learned what we thought was grass was really feed for Mr. Stoney's intriguing mule, named "Mule." Mr. Stoney's place was truly the very end of the town—incorporated and all. I don't remember a house being there on Mr. Stoney's land, just a barn where his mule was kept. In fact, a large open ditch bordered the southern tip of our community. Just like the famous northern border of our community, this drainage ditch, too, was becoming a sore spot about a lack of water drainage services to prevent flooding in the Low End community.

Mr. Stoney, who seemed older than dirt and sometimes talked to himself, fed the mule and lovingly brushed the animal's brown and black coat until it shone. I believe Mr. Stoney appeared to be at least 90 years old and he must have lived in his barn with his mule except for the nights we didn't see him returning home as he normally did by riding down South Chrisman Avenue Extended on the saddle-less back of the animal. In his generous moods, Mr. Stoney occasionally would attach a plow to a harness on his mule and help neighbors who didn't have access to a tractor prepare their gardens. He and his mule would plow row after row, breaking ground and readying the soil for planting. For that reason, the apparently wifeless and childless Mr. Stoney always had a meal from somebody's table. I don't think Muddear, Mrs. Margie or any of the ladies in the neighborhood cooked a Sunday or holiday meal without preparing an extra plate for Mr. Stoney.

When Southern, Illinois Central and other rail trains were not breezing by, the tracks were often our playgrounds and the best place in the world for harvesting the wild juicy blackberries Muddear used for baking buttery, syrupy sweet blackberry pie. Sometimes we would use the tracks for our races, too.

Tank, who was born to Mrs. Margie with an elephant leg, was two years older than me, but we were in the same class. He loved to run and always sprinted faster than any kid who lived in the Low End. Somehow, his one elephant leg seemed to give his body extra projection that propelled him into a kangaroo sort of bounce and at a gazelle kind of speed. He always won the races. In fact, I thought it was the loss of our schools that Tank never ran track. As tough as he was – and I mean he was a stone thug, Tank was probably too embarrassed to run track publicly for the school team in a school uniform. I did understand that since I, too, had to endure whispers and stares at my scarred face. Then again, we all had some kind of a physical challenge or flaw. What we didn't realize then as we were growing up, those challenges would make us stronger. Muddear told us time and time again, "If it doesn't kill you, it will make you stronger."

After the excitement of the races died down, the wild vineyards growing alongside the railroad tracks usually commanded our attention. Strawberries, blackberries, blueberries and grapes found their way into our bags, buckets or boxes and then on to our dinner tables as Sunday dessert in the lip-smacking, delicious buttery flaky crust of pies.

In my youth, it was a while before I learned a very important fact: when berries are plentiful, so are snakes. Earlier in the week, JoAnne, who lived behind the house near Mrs. Margie's café, encountered a snake as she headed to catch the morning school bus. JoAnne heard the rattler hissing and froze stiffly as the five foot long reptile rose up bearing venomous fangs in preparation to strike her. Her brother James, who kept a slingshot in his pocket, saw his sister in the midst of a life and death situation. Like David slew Goliath, but with much less fanfare, James cooed to his sister, saying, "Don't move." He took aim at the rattler with his wooden handled slingshot and a quarter-sized rock. Seconds after he pulled back the rubber sling, there was a soft "pop" and the rest of us waiting on the school bus watched in awe as the snake quickly slithered away from JoAnne. She remained voiceless and in shock. JoAnne missed school that day as she required bed rest to recuperate from her near death experience.

With the tale of JoAnne's rattler encounter circulating the neighborhood, rubber snakes started appearing everywhere – on the school bus, on the playground at school and even in a student's desk in the classroom. Bobby Randle was even brazened enough to put a rubber snake in our washing machine! Thinking he was going to scare the day lights out of me or my sister Malinda, he instead nearly gave Muddear a heart attack. Muddear discovered the very real looking fake snake amidst the wet laundry she was about to feed through the Speen Clean Washer wringer. Her scream could be heard across the Low End. Like JoAnne, Muddear took to bed rest.

Bobby, who never seemed to get over my sister popping him in the back with a dirty diaper, now had to suffer a serious whipping from his daddy. Mr. DeBoy wore Bobby's behind out with his fishing pole. When Mr. DeBoy finally stopped whipping Bobby, Mrs. Margie finished up the job with her three-hole leather strap. Even I felt sorry for Bobby – at least for a moment, but then I thought about how he scared my mother to nearly an early death. He deserved that double butt whipping, I sighed.

While picking berries on the railroad track, I decided that I could fill up my bucket a lot faster if I got away from the crowd who was lollygagging around after the race where Tank had once again left us all in his dust. I skipped up the track and found myself closer to the little hamlet of Boyle than I was to Cleveland. The bounty of blackberries hung heavy on their vines. Without thought to anything but the blackberry pies Muddear would make, I reached into the bushes and under vines to pluck the juiciest berries. With my bucket nearly full, I told myself that I would get a few more berries and head on back home.

Just as I reached for the black purple group of berries that almost touched the ground, I noticed a skinny blue-black snake aiming for a berry in the same bunch. I jumped back, kicked over my pale of sweet juicy berries and sprinted up the railroad track toward Cleveland. I was running so fast that in that moment I could have outrun Tank. I looked up from the tracks and saw the lights of a train speeding my way! I jumped from the railroad track, hopped over the ditch beside it and ran through the adjacent cotton field until I found myself in the middle of the road where Mr. Stoney's place was on one side and the Hole in the Wall was on the other. I was huffing and puffing as my lungs strained to pull in air. The Hole in the Wall was closed and I saw no sign of Mr. Stoney.

Had the nightclub been open, I would have run in there despite my not meeting the legal age requirement. Although I'd never ridden a horse, had Mr. Stoney's mule been around, I would have jumped on it and rode it like Roy Rogers on Trigger. Neither option existed. Distressed, I glanced back toward the track. Like beep, beep the Road Runner trying to escape the clutches of Wile E. Coyote, I saw what I believed was a blue runner snake with his head raised three feet from the ground and sliding on his tail fast forward toward me. Perhaps it was the stifling Delta heat or the lack of oxygen getting to my brains due to my high-speed sprint from the railroad track and through the cotton field. I don't know now and I didn't know then. Yet, I knew then that I had to gather up more steam because surely that snake was after me. I took off, jetting up Chrisman Avenue and into our asbestos gray fake brick wrapped house. I collapsed on the sofa.

"Where are the berries," my mother asked? Stuttering out the word, "snaaaaa, snaaaake," I couldn't say much else. About an hour later, Phyllis and Rena rushed in the house telling Muddear, "Look at all these berries we found. Somebody just left their bucket full of berries on the side of the track."

"Whenever Muddear made pie from those blackberries, I want some homemade, hand-churned, vanilla ice cream on top. Surely, I deserved it," I thought to my stuttering, speechless self.

Wild Hogs

Hunting and fishing were sports us Haynes girls never, ever got to experience while growing up in Cleveland. My brothers often came home from a trip to Grenada Lake where they hung out with Mr. Hawkins' boys. Mr. Hawkins was one of Daddy's two bosses in the trucking business. He owned the company that distributed Falstaff beer.

I don't remember Daddy going hunting or fishing, but he wasn't averse to his sons learning the skill. In fact, he even gave in to years of pleas and allowed "Santa" to bring a b-b gun to my baby brother Randy. Just a year younger than me, Randy was often called Daddy's favorite son. While learning to load the gun by reading the instructions, Randy accidentally shot me in the leg.

That wound is among my four childhood scars that I still find myself explaining to people today. The first one is my scarred right cheek that I scratched over the years to try to calm my itching eczema. The second one is the scar on my left eyebrow that I earned when I ran into a pile of dirt as I tried to escape my brother Philip's wrath after teasing him about having to work in the cesspool. Then there is the wound from Randy shooting me in the leg with his new b-b gun. Oh, the last one is a knot on my right foot that I gained while following my brother Sammy around.

Sammy was banging a Coca Cola bottle on the tall aluminum television antenna that ran up the side of our house and extended several feet above the roofline of the house. The antenna brought snowy black and white programming from two network stations into our home. We made the pictures living color when we taped sheets of magical red, blue and yellow film over the boxed floor model television. Frankly, as long as we could get a clear picture of the six o'clock news and soap operas as *Dark Shadows, General Hospital* and *All My Children* on weekdays, the funnies and *American Bandstand* on Saturdays and Billy Graham and Lawrence Welk on Sundays, our family was pretty satisfied with programming from the monster antenna.

Chards of the splattered glass from the busted Coke bottle landed in my foot. Sammy, just a year older than me, blamingly said, "I told you about following me around so much. See what you made me do. Daddy is going to kill me." Then he picked me up and carried me to the house where Muddear attended to the disaster. Muddear picked out what pieces of glass she saw, sanitized the bloody cuts and patched up my foot with white gauze and a tan flesh-colored tape. By the time Aunt Chicken made her "medical" rounds as a traveling nurse several days later to give me my weekly shot for calming my eczema, the cut on the top center of my foot had healed over anything Muddear didn't see in my foot. Aunt Chicken, and later Dr. Searcy, suspected a piece of glass was still in my foot, but paying for surgery to remove it was apparently out of the question.

While Sammy stopped banging glass bottles on poles, Randy didn't stop shooting things. In fact, today, years later, he remains an avid hunter. After accidentally shooting me in the leg, Randy became a better shooter with his b-b gun. His skill improved as he practiced by shooting bottles off a sawed off tree trunk. Then he advanced to shooting cans off the fence that separated our property from the Hurricane Club. The Hurricane Club faced South Chrisman Avenue Extended and the property on the lot behind the nightclub was home to a Mexican restaurant called the El Rancho. The restaurant faced U.S. Highway 61. Funny, I don't remember ever going inside that restaurant, but I do remember going to its back window ordering a dozen or two of greasy hot tamales for Muddear and some of her clients whose hair she was pressing or curling.

The only time the kitchen in our house wasn't in use for cooking was when Muddear used it to earn a few dollars styling hair. There she would sit on a wooden barstool that had a very worn green vinyl cushioned seat. Sitting in a dining room chair in front of the barstool would be one of Muddear's many regular clients who came in with hair looking like Don King's. For two dollars each, they left our house with an up do, a French roll, finger waves or some other style that rivaled any of the wigs that Diana Ross or the Supremes wore. The client's shoulders were draped with a large bath towel, protecting them from the hot irons and grease that sometimes splattered. Muddear would secure the towel around the client's neck with a wooden clothespin. With straightening combs, flat irons or curling irons smoking on one or two eyes of the gas stove, Muddear would deftly switch from one utensil to another, including a brush or a comb and alternate dabs of hair pomade with her fingertips on to her client's hair ends. "Fried, dyed and laid to the side" was a phrased that was surely coined by my mother and her clients, because we could hear the kinkiest of hair sizzle to a silky straightness when Muddear was working her magic. While "frying" came from the hot pressing irons, combs and curlers sizzling the hair and its oils, the "dyed "came from the many colorful hairstyles of the tresses of my mother and her clients.

Since Miss Clairol touted "blondes have more fun" on our black and white television and in our waited-for-with-baited-breath monthly copy of *Life Magazine*, Muddear really believed the ads. Much of her life, her tresses were blonde streaked, auburn, burgundy or red – any color but black, blue or gray. When she didn't have money for Miss Clairol's colors, Muddear mixed up her own coloring concoctions, usually peroxide was part of the base. Wanting to be like our Muddear, my sisters Malinda, Phyllis and I often fished out the discarded remnants of her chemical mixtures and applied them to our own hair. Our colorful streaks of hair were hidden by the thick black hair at our hairlines, however, when we were away from our mother or dad's watchful eyes, we would proudly part our hair to show off our blond streaks. Although we didn't get our hair fried much, we certainly sneaked in our versions of colorfully dyed or bleached hair.

One Saturday afternoon, Randy was out back practicing his shot with his new b-b gun when Muddear called from the kitchen for us to go to the the neighboring El Rancho to get her some hot tamales. For some unknown reason, Randy headed to the main entrance of the El Rancho restaurant. I ran to catch him to let him know what I assumed everyone knew – that he nor I could go through the El Rancho's front door. We had to go to the back window to place our order and wait for our hot tamales there. Randy, with fresh snowy black and white television memories of the episode that showed the night before with Sheriff Matt Dillon and his Deputy Chester pointing their rifles and guns to right a situation, thought he could do the same. He was so inflamed with anger to discover he could not be served in the front of the restaurant that he threatened to get his b-b gun to make the owners of the El Rancho do right by us. I ran back home to tell Muddear of Randy's plan. She dropped her curling irons and knocked over her entire set up as she ran outside to grab her nine-year-old baby boy, saving him from whatever harm that awaited him inside the front door of the El Rancho Mexican Restaurant. In her rush, Muddear knocked a sizzling hot straightening comb from the stove. It fell, just inches from my Godmother Mrs. Rosie's toweled shoulders to the linoleum floor. The hot comb burned straight through the floor covering, scorching the wood underneath.

Days later, a calm Randy finally got to use his b-b gun for some good causes. He shot birds that were stealing seeds from our garden that we had spent hours planting. He shot an occasional squirrel or rabbit that dared to be brave enough to run across our property. Smothered squirrel or stewed rabbit graced our table from time to time. For us, the meal was like having porterhouse steaks or chicken that we didn't have to figure out how to cut so everybody got a piece. Randy and my older brothers moved up to fishing and real hunting when they visited the Hawkins family at Grenada Lake. Sometimes they would bring home a deer, other times their catch would be fish – red bony snapper, tasty buffalo fish, bottom feeding catfish, succulent trout and the dreaded bitter-tasting gar fish. On a great fishing day, they brought home large red and white plastic Igloo coolers filled with a variety of fish. When deer meat was part of their loot, they came home with it already prepared for cooking or freezing. The fish was seldom dressed when we got to see it. All of us girls would spread out newspapers on a table outside. Then we would scale the fish, gut it and cut it for freezing or cooking – usually deep-frying.

On one particular hunting trip, the guys decided they were really going to bring home some bacon. They went hunting for wild hogs. Randy was the youngest of the group and knew little about hunting boars. He learned that nighttime was the best time for hunting these tough animals. The guys pitched their camouflaged viewing stand. They left Randy near their campsite as they went back to the truck to gather some traps and other gear.

The curious Randy, with a fully loaded .22 caliber rifle in hand, heard some squealing oink sounds and decided to check out the source. He glanced back at the path to the truck where the others seemed to be taking too long to return. Not wanting to miss his prospective catch, Randy ventured deeper into the woods toward the sound of the squeals. He stumbled upon several black and pink wild piglets apparently crying out for their mother. Randy turned around and saw a short, black-haired boar snorting steam from its pink nostrils as it barreled through the woods toward him. Despite having a loaded double-barreled Winchester rifle in his hands, Randy took off running.

About an hour later, when my brothers Terry, Lester, Philip and Sammy, and the two Hawkins brothers Ray and Kenny found my baby brother Randy, he was 14 feet above ground, perched in a tree, still holding on to his loaded rifle. Randy couldn't bring himself to shoot the boar that was waiting at the trunk of the tree for his debarkation. Randy felt the six baby pigs needed their parents to survive, so he wouldn't shoot the mad boar even if the hog wanted to kill him. Randy knew the hog had a family to take care of, so he wouldn't let the other guys shoot the wild hog either. Finally, the boys on the ground scared the boar away from the tree as they fired a few shots near the ground where the wiry haired black hog stood awaiting for Randy to come down from the tree. The stubborn animal trotted away from the tree and headed back to the baby pigs.

No bacon was to be had that week. However, the next week was hog-killing time. There would be bacon, crackling, ham, pork chops, chitterlings, hog maws, hog head souse, pig feet, pig tails, pork loins and more for smoking, curing, pickling or freezing to supplement the garden vegetables that would be canned or frozen to support the family through the lean winter months.

The easiest part was the capturing of the hogs – they were in a pigpen just a few yards from our house. While we loved the carnival like atmosphere of this special day, my siblings and I hated the actual hog-killing time or even the lesser eventful chicken-killing time. The killing part was gruesome. Seeing chickens run around with their heads cut off or their necks broken or bleeding until they died caused many nightmares for me. Any one of my brothers elected by Muddear to wring a chicken's neck and then chop it off was deemed cruel by us girls.

The sounds of dying hogs screaming were sure to bring on some sleepless nights. I couldn't bear to watch the process that usually included knocking the animal in the head and cleaning the hog's wiry hair from its body with scalding boiling water. These animals that we had fed and cared for and sometimes given pet names were going to be on our breakfast or dinner plates. Whenever chickens raised in our yard were on the dinner table as part of our meal, it didn't matter if it was smothered, baked, fried or barbecued, my sisters and I often became nauseated and had to leave the table. However, for our brothers, that meant more chicken for them to eat.

Somehow, we all got past eating bacon and ham that came from the hogs we raised. Maybe it was because we didn't spend as much time around the hogs as we did with the chickens. Meat from the farm-raised hogs was delicious, but, I never developed a palate for wild boar because it always seem to have a gamey taste. Yet, my brother Randy quickly got over his concern about wild hogs having families of little pigs who needed them. All Muddear had to do was to put a plate of barbecue boar ribs in front of Randy. He would devour the meat and then suck the marrow out of the bones in no time flat!

In fact, even us girls learned to appreciate the best part of hog-killing days. It was like the county fair had come to our front yard. Kids from all over the neighborhood stood in line to get a scoop of fresh crackling straight out of the large black deep frying kettle that stood over a big fire. The adult on fry duty would scoop out a basket full of crackling from the bubbling grease and drain it on newspapers covered with brown grocery bag paper. Special seasoning was sprinkled on the cubed pieces of hog skin as the kids lined up to get the freshest pork skins possible. After the bonus of getting our hot crackling, the 'games' followed. Playing cards, throwing horseshoes, jumping double-dutch ropes and riding inside of discarded thread bare tires from the 18-wheeler transportation trucks made for more excitement on hog-killing day.

The Wake

Sometimes the strangest of things can happen. One Friday afternoon, Mr. Friday dropped us off at the bus stop in front of our house a little later than normal. I ran into the house eager to share news with my big sister Malinda Jean about the day's basketball game at B.L. Bell Elementary School. Mr. Tharpe's sixth grade class played Mrs. Fairman's fifth graders on the school's only basketball court. Located on the school's playground, the dirt swepted court was flanked on each end with a bike tire rim that served as a basketball goal. Posted on poles, these goals did not allow for slam dunking. A year younger than most of my classmates, I scored 10 points and could barely wait to tell Malinda Jean that I used some of the hustling techniques she taught me. Blocking shots, stealing the ball and making layups (interpersed with much double-drilling, fouling and traveling calls) gave me hope for making the Trojanettes Basketball Team at East Side High School in a few years.

I ran through the house calling out "Jean, Jean, Jean!" With no answer, I bumped right into Grandmama Estella who promptly told me to stop running in the house. As I noticed the eerie quietness in the house, I realized Jean was not home, nor were Muddear and Daddy. In her seemingly always serious tone, Grandmama said "Hush up child. Your mama and daddy took Jean to the hospital."

Hospitals. Death. East Bolivar County Hospital located on Mississippi Highway 8 was a pretty scary place. Of course, my sister being at the hospital meant something was seriously wrong. Although it was a place where people got well, I was overwhelmed with the thought of hospitals being a place where people were in pain and where people go to die. Praises be and glory to God, my six-foot-tall, long legged and beautiful sister Malinda Jean did come home that following Sunday. However, she wasn't the same vibrant, funny, effervescent, happy sister who lived with us just days ago. She was different – withdrawn, under doctors' orders to stay in bed, and she had very little to say. That weekend and the week following were among the saddest of times we had in our Low End home.

The following Monday afternoon, when Mr. Friday pulled up the "big yellow dog" to our stop, a sleek black hearse brandishing the Brinson Funeral Home logo was rolling out of our long graveled driveway. Fear gripped my heart as my wobbly legs somehow carried me to lean on the lone flowering tree in our front yard. As I leaned on the mimosa tree that hung heavy with fuzzy pink tear drop like flowers, the thought of my beautiful sister Malinda Jean dead was overwhelming. I sank to my knees where the trunk of the mimosa tree gave me support. My younger siblings Randy, Phyllis and Florida Rena ran on into the house to see why the hearse was there.

Sister Ramsey from across the street came over to pull me up from the foot of the mimosa tree. "Girl, get up off that ground. Go in the house, your family needs you to be strong right now," she said as she pushed me toward the house. When I stepped inside the house, Grandmama, Muddear, Aunt Chicken and even my big sister Malinda were all there – alive! Thanking God for the miracle of life, it dawned on me that nobody was happy but me. Then I saw why.

A small white casket was sitting in Muddear and Daddy's bedroom, just off to the left of our family room. Through the open door, I saw the most beautiful baby in the world, dressed in a long white baptismal gown and lying in the casket on a bed of satin pink cushions like a sleeping baby doll. I learned later that the baby was my niece Geraldine. She died on Friday night as my sister Jean gave birth to her. Apparently, Malinda was given the wrong drug during labor. The drug caused an instant death for the new baby that was fighting her way into life.

Gave birth to a baby? When was Malinda pregnant? How did I miss knowing this? Daddy had such a tight rein on his kids, how did Malinda Jean even get to see a boy outside of school and church. What fool would risk his life by messing with L.D. Haynes' beautiful daughter? In the weeks following, the answers came trickling in. My teenage sister had met and fallen for a teacher from Shaw High School while playing basketball for the East Side High School Trojanettes. The teacher took advantage of her innocence. I don't know what Daddy did about the teacher. All I know is we never heard of him again. It seemed like he disappeared from the face of the Delta.

For a full week, the little dead body of my baby-doll looking niece laid in the open casket in my parents' bedroom. Every day, there were visitors who came by to look at Geraldine and to pray for her soul and our family. On the second night, when everyone was sleep, I tip-toed into the master bedroom turned temporary funeral parlor to see if Geraldine was real or just a baby doll in a casket. As I touched the black curly tendrils of hair on her head, I whispered "wake up baby girl." Emboldened, I let my fingers slide down her closed eyes and onto her cheeks. The clammy, coldness of her skin freaked me out. "So this is what death feels like," I thought as I eased out of the room and found my way through teary eyes to the girls' bedroom in the back of our house. After a few sleepless nights, Saturday morning came with the presence of a lot of pomp and circumstance. The pastor from St. Peter's Rock Church, where my mother and my sister Malinda worshipped, came by to eulogize Geraldine. The entire family, including Daddy, gathered in the family room to say our goodbyes to the precious baby who never knew life outside her mother's womb.

Once again, the Brinson Funeral Home hearse pulled into our driveway. Instead of bringing a dead body into our home, the staff of two black-suited, white-gloved funeral directors came inside. They ceremoniously closed the casket with my niece's body inside of it. They lifted the casket and marched in timed steps to place the casket inside the hearse. We all followed the hearse to a small graveyard located near the Southern end of Chrisman Avenue, just behind the Hole in the Wall nightclub.

The preacher prayed again, mumbled something about ashes to ashes and dust to dust prior to giving my sister Malinda Jean a bouquet of flowers. She solemnly sprinkled the flowers over the casket that held her daughter's lifeless little body. As we all walked away, I heard the grave diggers dumping clumps of dirt over the casket. I stopped and cried to seemingly deaf ears, "We can't leave Geraldine in this graveyard. She will get cold at night. We can't leave her."

"Hush, child. She is in heaven with God, now," Grandmama Estella said as she wrapped one arm around my shoulder and nudged me past the Hole in the Wall, on to Chrisman Avenue and home.

The Morning Bench

The United Missionary Baptist Church, under leadership of the colorful Rev. Sammie Lee Rash, was located on the corner of White Street and Chrisman Avenue, just outside the incorporated city limits of Cleveland. The church was exciting, unlike my mother's old fashioned St. Peter's Rock Missionary Baptist Church where women couldn't even wear pants inside the sanctuary and certainly not as stiff as the upper crusted St. Paul's Church where most of the teachers from H.M. Nailor Elementary and East Side High schools attended.

There, saying "Amen" aloud or waving hands in the air as praise would get anyone who dared to do so stares that would make him or her want to leave or slide under the pew. The new brick worship center of United Baptist, with its shiny Old English polished pews, spirited-filled choir led by Big Milton and the dapper young Pastor Rash, became the church home for most of the young folks who lived on the Low End. For that matter, it became known as the church for young folks throughout the Cleveland area.

Pastor Rash was not the Bible-thumping, brimstone and fire preacher who just threatened us with God's wrath. No, he was warm, personable and real in his messages to us. His story-weaving gave analogies like Jesus did – bringing home to even us children the messages about the perils of lying, cheating, stealing, drinking, pre-marital sex, killing, lusting, jealousy, adultery, murder, coveting, gluttony, other immoralities, sins and general violations of God's commandments to His people. The slim, six-foot-plus tall minister of the Gospel planted and nourished the seeds of salvation in the heads and hearts of most who heard him. In the midst of his sermons on God's goodness and how God sacrificed his own son Jesus so that we could have everlasting life, Rev. Rash gave us visions of entering the pearly gates, walking on streets paved of gold, our heavenly mansions, no pain, no ailments, no poverty and even no grudge ditch!

With perfect diction and oftentimes a long, drawn out word or phrase, Rev. Rash would start his sermon slow and even. As his momentum started to build, his sermon would go in to a frenzy of whooping and hollering until he was dripping wet with sweat and gasping for air. Big Milton, who doubled as the church pianist as well as choir director, would add a crescendo of music to the message, usually a song supporting the sermon. All around the church, the congregation would be singing, shouting, dancing and feeling the Spirit take over their being. Fans brandishing Brinson's Funeral Home were passed around to help cool and calm down the overheated congregation. However, the sermons were never complete unless some wayward soul, a deeply hurting parishioner or a mother or two fainted and their seemingly lifeless bodies had to be taken out of the church by ushers dressed in crisp white nurse-like uniforms. More times than not, a few deacons would have to step in to lift the blanket draped women off the church floor. They would put displaced wigs and hats on the women's chest and carry the limp bodies into the nurse's room where the women were revived with a sniff of ammonia infused smelling salts.

Other deacons or assistant pastors, acting like Maceo Parker supporting the Godfather of Soul in a James Brown concert, cloaked our perspiration-drenched pastor with a black cape. Then, the reverend would ease from the pulpit to his office through a right exit behind the choir stands. He must have had a complete bathroom with a shower back there. After the choir sang a couple more selections and a few of the singers fainted or cried or testified about how God had delivered them from something, a fresh Pastor Rash stepped back into the pulpit. If he left the pulpit in a drenched yellow polyester knit suit, he came back in a lime green, hot pink or even red bell-bottomed polyester suit that was complemented with a matching tie, shirt, socks and shoes. In fact, our pastor's attire could put Superfly's wardrobe to shame. Surely, we would get to see at least two of his high-fashioned suits on any given Sunday. In his second suit, Pastor Rash would proceed to "open the doors of the church" to anyone who didn't have a church home, who wanted to accept God's free gift of salvation by getting baptized or to join United Baptist so that they could develop a closer relationship with the Lord. Many accepted his invitation, including my sisters Toni, Rena and Phyllis and me.

For a couple of years before we joined United Baptist, we ditched my parents' church of St. Peter's Rock and on a regular basis attended the church of our choice – the one led by the dynamic Pastor Rash. Most Sundays, many of us from the Grudge Ditch Gang would be up early, dressed and ready to walk the mile or so up Chrisman Avenue – past the 400 Club, past the Swing Out Club, past Nell's Barbershop and Mr. Ben's Cleaners and on up to United Baptist.

Sunday school started at 9 a.m. If we found ourselves late, some of us would hitch a ride by piling into Mrs.

Margie's big old Chevy Impala. Other Sundays, Mrs. Inez, on her way to the Methodist church, would give us a ride in her sleek Continental that had soft as butter burgundy leather seats. Also, from time to time, Mrs. Cleo, who picked Muddear up to join her for services at St. Peter's Rock, would avail to us the back seat of her prissy neat gold AMC Rambler. Muddear and Mrs. Cleo would drop us off at United Baptist and continue on Chrisman Avenue to Ruby Street. There, they served as mothers and on the first Sunday of each month, wore white dresses or suits with white handkerchiefs or fancy hats pinned to their heads and white stockings, shoes and gloves. Every Sunday, they sat in the special section reserved for the highly esteemed church mothers at the front of St. Peter's Rock sanctuary.

If we arrived at United Baptist early, we'd skip across Chrisman Avenue to the "green" store, which was not unlike the "pink" store in our previous uptown neighborhood. Although our bellies were full from a breakfast of pancakes and sausages or grits and salmon patties, my friends and I, as most kids at church, could not resist the lure of goodies inside the "green" store. Jolly Ranchers, Red Hots, Cracker Jacks, bubble gum, jelly beans, Tootsie Rolls, peppermint sticks, Jaw Breakers, Lollipop Suckers, Goo-Goo Patties, PayDays and more were ours to be had for as much as our nickel or quarter would buy. Many times, our pockets and small purses overflowed with candy, especially when we decided we needed the candy more than United Baptist needed our tithes of a dime or a quarter. Despite believing that not tithing would reduce our bountiful blessings because doing so was like stealing from the Lord, Mr. Le, proprietor of the "green" store, ended up with many dimes that were supposed to go to the support of United Missionary Baptist Church. Thank God, the church did not depend on the tithing of the Grudge Ditch children for its survival!

Although we were church-going kids, Mr. Le brought out his wife, mother, father, son and daughter to help guard their stock from sticky fingers and watch the activity in the store when the Grudge Ditch Gang and the rest of the Low End kids piled in trying to get one last sugar rush before having to sit through Sunday school and church from 9 a.m. until 2 p.m.

The green store, unlike the pink store, never had a problem from me. The one time in my life that I was brazen enough to steal happened when I lived uptown on Roosevelt Street. Just five years old, I took the dare from my friends Shirley and Colleen Carter and stole a bag of finger-licking-good, salty Lay's potato chips from the "pink" store. That nickel's worth of theft caused me weeks of pain. Muddear made me take the half-eaten bag of chips back to the store, confess the theft, face possible imprisonment at the county jail or the dreaded Parchman

Prison Farm of the Mississippi State Penitentiary (so I worried at the time) and she made me pay for the greasy chips, too. Upon my return home, she sent me out back to pick a green, flexible switch from one of the branches on the plum tree that grew in our small back yard on Roosevelt Street. Muddear, who seldom administered corporal punishment to us kids because she usually saved it for Daddy to handle, gave me a pretty good spanking with that switch. In between licks, she preached to me the entire session. "Don't you know liars steal? God says a liar can't tarry in His sight. God does not like liars. If you have been stealing, you've been lying. If you lie, you will steal. If you steal, you will kill. I will be doggone if I am going to raise a liar, thief and murderer in my house," Muddear exclaimed. For good measure, just in case the 10 lashes didn't beat the potential for evil out of me, I was grounded for the rest of the month.

Frankly, a few days after Muddear worked her magic on me, I actually saw some good in the whole ordeal. I was happy to be grounded because I realized that Muddear didn't tell Daddy that I was a thief in the making. Either that, or Daddy figured Muddear handled the situation as well as he would have. For sure, my siblings and I would choose Muddear's discipline over Daddy's discipline any day of the week. Years later, my younger sister Toni was being joshed about her "goody-two-shoe" personality. She laughed, "I saw all those whippings you all were getting and decided I didn't want any part of it. I was scared straight as a toddler. Being good was a much better alternative than suffering the punishment you all got."

When my younger sisters and I decided the Lord had called us to join United Baptist, Muddear sat us down to ascertain that we were not just following our friends. Daddy, who didn't go to church much lately anymore, joined in the questioning. (He stopped going to church shortly after some of the folks at St. Peter's Rock solicited him to be their pastor. He declined, saying, "I'm not crazy enough to play with God on something so serious. Pastoring these 13 children has my hands full.")

"How do you know it was God who called you to join church? What do you know about God? How do you know it was God talking to you and not the devil? Would you join if Florida Mae and Shirlene were not joining? When was the last time you read your Bible? Are you ready to confess your sins and turn away from wickedness?" We skated through the interview. Muddear and Daddy probably had a laugh or two about us when they were alone; after all, four of their youngest children getting baptized was a good deal for them. We would be more involved in wholesome holy activities and the fear of God, along with more knowledge about doing right versus wrong would lighten their burden of raising so many children in a world filled with sin and sinfully temptations.

The June revival at United Baptist kicked off with a big time preacher from Chicago. I don't remember his name, but to us, he was like the famous Rev. Ike on steroids. The preacher mesmerized the members of United as well as many of the visitors who came from across the Delta to ignite a spiritual fire in their own lives. No one felt the summer heat as the visiting preacher belted out songs and sermons. My sisters, several others from the Grudge Ditch community and I were among the sinners sitting on the first rows of pews at the front of the church. The "morning" bench many times felt like the "mourning" bench and other times was clearly the "moaning" bench as all eyes were regularly directed toward us, the new recruits. Surely, we mourned and moaned beneath the gazes of the saints. The females donned white dresses and the males all wore white shirts with dark pants. That Chicago preacher worked his heart out as he tried to preach Satan out of us and to get other unconfessed sinners to "fess up" and join the rest of us on the morning bench. That week, some 30 of us joined United Baptist, making it the fastest growing church in the Bolivar County.

On wobbly legs and weak knees, I went before the congregation and said my name. I told Pastor Rash and the United congregation that I believe in the Trinity. I said I believe God is the maker and master of the universe, that God's Son Jesus is the Christ who died on the cross for my sins, that Jesus was raised from the dead and that the Holy Spirit is my Comforter. I said I believe I will live in heaven with God. I did not say the rest of what I was thinking – "The main reason I am joining this church, wearing this white dress and sitting on that morning bench facing those inquisitive and sometimes accusatory stares is because I want to hang out with my friends. Oh yes, the other reason is the fear of God is in me. I don't want to die and go to hell. I have come close to fire. It is hot. I don't even want to imagine living in hell's fires for eternity. I am having a hard time imagining living in the hot Mississippi Delta heat for the rest of my natural life."

Seven days later, from the Sunday that I went before the church to confess my love for God, my sisters and I lined up at 7 a.m. to get baptized. The saints in my family, especially Muddear, Grandmama Estella and my older sister Malinda, were happy. I was scared almost out of my wits. The baptism pool at United was built into the wall like an upper room, a few feet above the center of the choir stands that were behind the pulpit.

In rubber boots that came past his waist, Pastor Rash awaited us in the several feet of cold water in the baptism pool. In the line before me, over and over, Pastor Rash dunked person after person in the water as he said some holy magical words and the choir sang out "Wade in the Water Children." When I arrived at the edge of the pool dressed in a long white robe that I believed was made from a bed sheet, I hesitantly stepped into the water and turned around so Pastor Rash could put one of his arms behind my back and position his other hand to cover my nose and mouth. I heard him say something like, "I baptize you in the name of the Father, Son and Holy Spirit..." Without any further notice, he pushed me back and dunked me into the cold water. The white rubbery swim cap fell off my head. I came up kicking and fighting the water and choking and spitting out mouthfuls of water that almost drowned me.

As Pastor Rash regrouped, he hurried me out of the pool to the awaiting towels held by ushers and church mothers. I didn't look back to check on my younger sisters who were up next for the washing away of their sins. As I waddled forward to the awaiting church mothers and ushers with the dry towels, I wondered if the washing of my sins needed a "do over." If I choked that much, people are going to say I wasn't saved. Amidst my thoughts of doubt, I found encouragement. In my waterlogged ears, I heard the choir crooning, "It chilled my body, but not my soul." Then, as they swayed to the alluring singing, I waded my way out of the pool to dry towels and living a life secured by God's salvation.

Finally, the long day gave me the one song I waited to hear Big Milton and the choir sing. When all of us new converts felt our bodies syncopating to the beat of "Get Right Church and Let's Go Home," my blood sisters Toni,

Phyllis and Florida Rena, along with several of our Grudge Ditch Gang sisters and brothers, joyously celebrated surviving the salvation ritual. We headed home to one of the best Sunday dinners ever – collard greens with ham hocks, crackling cornbread, candied yams, macaroni and cheese casserole, smothered fried corn, hot yeast rolls, pot roast and peach cobbler.

Culture

The most culturally refined lady in our Grudge Ditch community was Mrs. Josephine Walker, a music teacher at B.L. Bell Elementary School and the pianist for the uptown Greater Solomon Chapel African Methodist Episcopal Church. In the minds of the kids in our community, Mrs. Walker was the wealthiest woman we knew. (I felt fortunate because she was a relative of sort – her daughter was once married to my mother's brother. As the story goes, Uncle Charlie and Miss Juanita eloped to California, never looking back to the Delta. Despite their not having any children together and their divorce and subsequent marriages to other people, the Walkers remained our cousins and my mother's in-laws of sort.)

My oldest sister Malinda had the gift of music. She could play the piano a little and was a true songbird. I felt Langston Hughes wrote his famous poem, "When Melinda Sings" with my sister's voice in mind. My sister Malinda Jean always led songs in the church and high school choirs. From time to time, she was the lead singer in a girls' group that she and a few of her friends formed. Perhaps I was biased, but I thought Malinda could sing as well as or better than a lot of the ladies I heard singing on the radio and television, including Diana Ross and the Queen of Soul Aretha Franklin. Like I said, I was biased when it came to my big sister. Mrs. Walker tried to teach me to sing with hope against hope that I, too, had the voice that Malinda had. She was sorely disappointed.

Finally accepting that the singing genes Malinda had were not passed on to me, Mrs. Walker decided she would teach me (and her granddaughter Rosemary) how to play the piano. I would walk up Chrisman Avenue, turn left on Winnie Lane past the 400 Club and past the graveyard until I reached the dirt road where the Walker's big two story white mansion loomed up from the dust. At least, the big house seemed like a mansion to us. Its big wrap around porch was perfect for lazy afternoons hanging out with my cousin Rosemary in big wooden rocking chairs or swinging benches suspended from the ceiling over the porch. In the front parlor stood an oak colored Chickering baby grand gold lettered piano. The short, stocky Mrs.

Walker, with her silky straight blue hair pinned neatly in a chignon at the nape of her neck, was often found sitting at the piano playing various church tunes. A few hours each week, she would explain and demonstrate the tones made by the various black and white piano keys to Rosemary and me. Much to the chagrin of the kind and very patient Mrs. Walker, was her eventual acceptance that I was tone deaf and she would get no more out of me than a few notes of "Twinkle, Twinkle, Little Star" and "Wade in the Water Children."

Although she gave up developing my musical talents, Mrs. Walker didn't give up on my cultural education. The perfectly beautiful hardwood floors throughout the Walker home guided me in the matron's effort to teach me to walk gracefully. With a book atop my head, I would walk back and forth throughout their house, trying to stay within the lines of a select two of the glossy floor planks. Since I couldn't look down, Rosemary would yell "out" every time I stepped out of the margin. At every "out," the book would shift into a downslide from my head. Then it would be Rosemary's turn to walk the planks with the thick leather bound "M" Britannica Encyclopedia on her head. For months, this little game that Mrs. Walker encouraged us in helped Rosemary and me stand straight, pull our shoulders back for a walk of pride as we held our heads up high. The two of us started to think that we could make it in the fashion industry, Rosemary as a designer and I as a model. (In fact, later in life, Rosemary joined me at the University of Southern Mississippi where I studied journalism and modeled some on one of the extracurricular organization's fashion teams. Rosemary earned her degree in fashion design, but ended up making a career as an officer in the Air Force.)

One of our teachers laughed when she heard that Mrs. Walker was trying to teach me some culture. "The only culture that child is gonna learn is agriculture," predicted the teacher about my future. She was somewhat on target because the agriculture beat was one of the main areas I covered during my time as a news reporter.

The widow of a husband who not only left her with a big home, Mrs. Walker owned much of the property in the southwestern part of the Grudge Ditch community. Acres and acres of land belonged to her, including my little hide out in the woods and the cotton field that covered several blocks along side of a section of Chrisman Avenue Extended.

When farming got to be too much for her to handle, she sold several acres of her land for a housing development project and even some to Rev. J.W. Fairman, who continued to farm cotton in a few blocks along Chrisman Avenue. Rev. Fairman and his wife (who was my fifth grade teacher) had as many children as my parents. Actually, they had more, edging us out with 14 children versus Muddear and Daddy's 13. Mrs. Walker's daughter Dot had five and it seemed that everybody who moved into the new housing development on either side of Chrisman Avenue had bunches of children or "chullen" as Grandmama Estella would say.

A sophisticated refined lady knows how to set a table, make a bed and keep an organized, clean house, Mrs. Walker explained to Rosemary and me. According our mentor, just as important as taking care of the home, is taking care of yourself. Keeping our clothes and hair neat was a high priority, she explained, and I cringed trying to figure how was I going to be as neat as Mrs. Walker if I was going to hang out with my brothers or play basketball, dodge ball and softball. What was I going to do about my private dirt floor hangout in the woods? I left the Walkers' house despondent that evening but committed to learning something about how to be a sophisticated, refined young lady.

When I arrived home, Daddy was cutting my brothers' hair. They lined up by the dining room table and one by one he shaved their heads with his electric clippers. After my youngest brother Randy hopped out of the chair, I hopped in. Daddy laughed as I begged him to cut my hair, too. To appease me, he decided he would just line up the edges on the nape of my neck. Before he knew it, his hand slipped and he had cut a wide swath from the neckline and across the side of my head! As my wavy black and streaks of peroxide bleached blond hair fell to the floor, Muddear walked into the room and screamed at the horror she saw. She snatched me up from the chair and shouted "L.D., have you lost your mind?" My beautician mother examined my disastrous haircut and decided to cut off the remainder of my once shoulder length hair. "If we just cut the rest off, it will grow back even," said my distraught mom. It grew in short spurts but never to the healthy rich mane I had before Daddy's accidental scalping of my head. In fact, later, one teacher remarked to me, "I can't believe your mother is a beautician. You come to school every day with such a nappy-looking head." I told Muddear what the teacher said. The next week, I was sporting a scalp burning, chemical permanent by Lustre Silk hair relaxer, with lye and all, that would make Mrs. Walker proud and shut down negative remarks about my mama's skills as a hairdresser.

Pierced ears became all the rave in Cleveland. NuNu, Mr. DeBoy's oldest daughter and my playmate, too, assured several of us that she could pierce ears. One night, she pierced her sister Yvonne's ears. A few days later, we saw Yvonne with broom straws in her ear lobes. She proudly pranced before us, showing off her newly pierced ears and the loops with which she had that would replace the straws in a couple of weeks. "Did it hurt," we asked. "Naw, it was a little prick and then it was over," she grinned.

Several of us went in search of NuNu, ready to get

holes in our ear lobes. Did we ask our parents? I don't think so. We made appointments for the next day. We all sat around the metal legged, blue Formica topped table in their kitchen. NuNu had her wares laid out – sewing needles, white thread, a metal tray of ice cubes, Vaseline Petroleum Jelly, cotton balls, Diamond matches, alcohol and straws from the broom. Like a surgeon, NuNu was meticulous. She had a broken piece of silver-backed glass that served as a hand mirror and she had an ink pen.

When I sat on the floor between her knees, she pulled my head back and with the Bic pen marked a blue dot on each of my ear lobes. She handed me the mirror and said, "Is this where you want the holes to go?" As I affirmed that she had correctly marked the target for her needle, NuNu proceeded to press an ice cube on each side of my ear lob. When I thought she had frozen the right side of my face, she swabbed my ear lobe with an alcohol laden cotton ball. She struck a match and held the number 10 size-sewing needle's point to the fire until the needle turned red hot. NuNu threaded the needle, wiped it with alcohol and told me to hold my breath. She STABBED my ear with the needle and a piercing murderous scream came from my mouth and a watershed of tears fell down my face. She put more alcohol and ice on my ear. As I cried like a baby, NuNu and the others tried to coax me into getting my other ear pierced, saying, "You can't walk around with just one ear pierced." I thought about it for a while and conceded that one pierced ear would not fit into Mrs. Walker's definition of refinement.

Despite the two aspirins I accepted from NuNu and swallowed to relieve some of my pain, I slept fitfully that night. The next morning, just like Yvonne, I proudly went out to show off my broom straw filled earlobes. My sister Phyllis woke up with fevered, keloid-swollen ears and a trip to Dr. Searcy's office. When my ears healed from the pain of being stabbed with a needle, I felt blessed that I didn't have keloids like my sister. I was more blessed when Mrs. Walker gave me my first pair of earrings. They were tiny diamond studs.

Martin, Fannie & Us

There was a strange air across the Mississippi Delta in the mid- to late 1960s. Oppressors and the oppressed were no longer pretending to see eye to eye about economics, civil rights and the deep South's way of life. The Freedom Riders had come along to inspire many of us throughout the Delta about equal access and opportunities to lift ourselves up out of poverty.

The Black Panthers had swooped through downtown and the back alleys of downtown Cleveland. A path of fire and destruction were left, including the torching of our beloved "pink" store that was on Ruby Street, just across from St. Peter's Rock Missionary Baptist Church and Louie Block's Service Station/L.D.'s Mechanic Shop.

A spark from the fire set at the "pink" store leaped over

to the service station, starting an inferno of heat that left the service station, mechanic shop and the neighboring church's parsonage in cinders and ashes.

People across America were watching the South and especially the Mississippi Delta. It seemed to be a hot bed of emotional frenzy at the heart of the civil rights struggle. Dr. Martin Luther King, Jr. was coming to Memphis, just an hour north of Cleveland to kick off his non-violence campaign to help the sanitation workers in Memphis gain job equity and fairness. Dr. King's inspiring messages were moving the most humble of people to impact changing America's racial discrimination policies and Jim Crow laws that proliferated in Mississippi and in most other Southern states.

Mrs. Margie's cousin, Mrs. Fannie Lou Hamer of Ruleville, Mississippi, lived just eight miles east of Cleveland. She was busy trying to enlighten the area's sharecroppers about how to get a fairer deal for their labor. Many days, when she visited Mrs. Margie and Mr. DeBoy or when Mrs. Margie gathered up her girls and usually me, too, for a ride to visit Mrs. Fannie Lou in her small Ruleville home, we heard about the horrors of injustice going on around us.

Hundreds of Freedom Riders arriving in the Mississippi Delta was fresh on the minds of many Clevelanders. Our cousin Sam Block (from Uncle Louie's side of the family) was one of the local leaders in the Student Non-Violent Coordinating Coalition (SNCC) who was working to organize voter registration drives in the Delta. During one march, a rally of protesters was disbursed when police shot into the crowd. Sam was hit, taken to East Bolivar Hospital and immediately released by the medical folks there who said Sam was without injury. Fortunately, Sam had Aunt Chicken as a nurse who treated him for his wound. Sam didn't give up on the fight to change things in the Delta. In the months and years that followed, Sam joined others in the fight for civil rights for all Mississippi Deltans.

One suffocating and stifling hot day in May, Joetha Collier was leaving the Ruleville Auditorium where her Drew High School graduation class was reveling in the commencement theme of "Make America A Better Place." Still donned in her graduation cap and gown and clutching her freshly received diploma to her chest, Joetha stepped out to face her new world as a graduate bound for a degree in teaching at the nearby Mississippi Valley State College (now a university) in Itta Bena. As Joetha breathed in the air of hope and a new America, a pickup truck full of rowdy men drove by, and one of them shot Joetha in the head as Joetha 's classmates scattered and fell to the concrete veranda to dodge the bullets of racial hate.

U.S. Senator Edmund Muskie later described the tragedy: "Last Tuesday night…there was another commencement for a small high school in Drew, Mississippi. At the end of the ceremony, where the graduates were told to "make America a better place," 18-year-old Joetha Collier was killed by a sniper…. No one knows why Miss Collier was singled out. There were only two things about her that most people noticed after she was murdered.... She was clutching her diploma in her left hand – and she was black.... Now she is dead – and so is the once distant dream.... What has happened to America – when some men decide to take out their hate on teenagers and children? ...What will be left of the American future if we continue to endure the random and wanton killing of innocents? ...The story is on page 1, then on page 9, and finally it is not mentioned at all. Buried in a past we cannot change and want to ignore, the last tragedy is forgotten until the next tragedy shocks us again."

The pain of the violence and hate that stole Joetha's life haunted the Grudge Ditch Gang and much of our community. Much of the Low End communities, including all of the original Grudge Ditch Gang's families, joined Mrs. Hamer and people from all over the Delta and probably from all over the nation at Drew High School's gymnasium for Joetha's funeral. (Most people know of the high school because it produced the famed professional football player Archie Manning of the Ole Miss Rebels and later, the New Orleans Saints. I knew it for Joetha and her graduation death that opened my eyes to the pain and frustration of growing through hatred from which people all around me were suffering.)

Joetha's was the first funeral I'd attended since being baptized at United Baptist. I kept wondering why the preacher didn't just lay his hands on Joetha's body and raise her up out of that heavy, flora-laden casket. All he had to do was to command death to leave Joetha's body, just like Jesus did for Lazarus, I thought.

The next week, my brother Lester was delivered home by the local police to Daddy. The officer told Daddy that Lester was in downtown Cleveland, marching with the civil rights folks. "I know how you keep your boys in line, so I thought I would bring him to you instead of taking him to jail," he explained. In our hushed house, Daddy gave Lester a good talking to. It did not take effect. The next week, Daddy was summoned to the Sunflower County Jail that held my brothers Sammy and Lester, as well as many other members of the Grudge Ditch Gang. Mrs. Hamer and a number of other members protesting the injustice of the sheriff's office not doing more about Joetha's murder were there at the jail, too.

According to Sammy, who was sporting the new look of braids, Mrs. Hamer and several of the other civil rights workers had advised them that they would be arrested. They wanted the children who were ages 12 or so to join hands and make human chains as they marched in front of the courthouse and segregated businesses such as restaurants. They knew the police would not try to keep the children in jail. However, they also knew the police would arrest and hold the older folks, including the kids who were nearing 17 and 18 years of age since the laws allowed them to be tried as adults. They gave the girls extra warnings, too, because horrible things were done to the girls who were arrested and being jailed during the protests.

On this particular march, when Mrs. Hamer and many members of the Grudge Ditch Gang were arrested along with a few hundred other protesters, the police separated the adults from the children and then the males from the females. Somehow, because Sammy had braids, the policemen shuffled him into the jail cell with the girls. Five hours later, Sammy was a happy camper as Daddy arrived to retrieve him, my brother Lester and some of the other members of the Grudge Ditch Gang from jail. It was the one time Sammy preferred facing Daddy's punishment than possibly having to face a bunch of hateful police if he had to try to protect the girls in the jail cell with him from the police's abuse.

The truck load of murderers who did the drive by shooting that killed Drew High's Joetha were boasting about their "kill." That's how the protesters saw things. Years later, here are excerpts of a court record detailing the murder in the case of Wesley Parks v. the State of Mississippi: "The appellant, indicted and tried for murder, was found guilty of manslaughter in the Circuit Court of Sunflower, Mississippi, and sentenced to 20 years imprisonment in the state penitentiary at Parchman, Mississippi. From that verdict and sentence, Parks appealed to the court:

"...the appellant, his wife and infant son and 18-year-old

nephew, Allen Wilkerson, a co-indictee, drove to Drew from their Memphis home. Appellant and Wilkerson drank four quarts of beer prior to leaving ...around 4 p.m. They drank another can of beer before arriving at the home of his brother, Wayne Parks, another co-indictee. The appellant, Wayne and Allen went into Drew, drank more beer....flashed a pistol and made unfriendly remarks to a group of colored boys.... appellant pointed a .22 caliber pistol out the window and fired one shot. The bullet hit and killed Miss Joetha Collier, an 18-year-old female..."

My brothers and several of the neighborhood children were released from jail into Daddy's custody. They, nor the other protesters under the age of 16, were never charged with disturbing the peace or unlawful gathering. Even Florida, my playmate wound up in jail as part of the protest. Somehow, Florida found herself with her "Cousin Fannie Lou," and a host of other relatives and neighbors preparing to march in Ruleville. One of the civil rights workers complained to Mrs. Hamer that they had a short, stocky dark girl in the group who claimed she was 12, but because of her physical attributes, he didn't think she was 12. She was short enough to be nine or so. Her chest looked like that of an adult. Maybe she was older. He was confused. "Dat gum it," Mrs. Hamer proclaimed, "If she says she is 12, then she is 12. Let her march!"

After the group was released from jail, Mrs. Hamer saw Florida, who was certainly not yet 12 years of age.

The civil rights activist let out a guffawed laughter as she grabbed her little cousin. "Hell girl, your boobs are bigger than mine. No wonder they thought you were older than 12." The whole group fell out laughing as Florida walked proudly among them in making her first mark in the fight for civil rights.

While the nation was brewing over civil rights, Daddy and Terry, another one of my older brothers, also had a falling out about parental rights and the individual rights of young adults. The two of them were standing near the back door of our home. I was coming out of the girls' bedroom and shocked speechless as I heard Terry say to Daddy, "You can't stop me. I am going to the protest." The next thing I heard was Daddy hitting Terry up side his head. I didn't get the details of the argument, but even I knew that it was a death wish to talk back to Daddy.

Terry left the house to cool off. He came back the next day, packed a bag of clothes and announced that he was dropping out of Mississippi Delta Junior College where he was studying architectural design. Terry was one of the 50 young black students tapped to be bussed every week day to integrate the historically racially segregated junior college that was located in Morehead, just 30 miles southeast of Cleveland. Frankly, Terry was barely 18 and getting weight-of-the-world kind of pressures from every side.

At home, my parents, grandmother, aunts and uncles

wanted Terry to represent his race in a positive way. The pastor, deacons, trustees, mothers and folks from his church family of St. Peter's Rock wanted my brother to be like Dr. Martin Luther King, Jr., by turning the other cheek and remaining non-violent as he was verbally and physically attacked in his daily trek to Mississippi Delta Junior College. Of course, many of Terry's high school buddies were pushing him to physically fight back when the bitter and hateful segregationists attacked him. No doubt, my brother had a heavy load.

Consequently, amidst all the pressure in the local fight for civil rights and the looming war in Vietnam, Terry signed up to join the Navy. Apparently, there was not much Daddy could do about Terry's actions. Upon his completion of basic training, the Vietnam War, which Dr. King and many others were protesting about, was my brother Terry's immediate destination. Shortly afterward, Lester took off for the Job Corps where he studied for an apprenticeship in mechanical engineering. Then, my brother Philip was drafted to serve his country – where he too would be Vietnam-bound.

I could see the worry lines increase in Daddy's forehead. In my mind, here was the smartest man in the world – who should have been president instead of John Fitzgerald Kennedy, Lyndon Baines Johnson or Richard Nixon – struggling with how to keep his sons safe from potential death. War in Vietnam and the ever-increasing struggle for civil rights in America made for many sleepless nights for

Daddy and many of the family leaders in Cleveland's Low End, across the town and across the Mississippi Delta.

Even with his older sons moving into adulthood where they would make and be responsible for their own decisions, Daddy still had several more children at home who needed his guidance. While it was difficult seeing his boys leave home, he was achieving his mission of making his children independent and self-sufficient. In the meantime, Daddy, Cleveland's resident civil rights activists Mr. Amzie Moore, Mr. Roosevelt Grenell and a host of other men continued to make their appeals to the town and county government for improved services to the people on the Low End. Mr. Moore pointed out to the federal government that town officials continued to gerrymander the precinct voting lines and use other illegal and unethical tactics so that blacks had little or no chance of being elected to town, county or state government, despite Bolivar County's majority black population. The U.S. Department of Justice finally mandated that the county must come up with a fairer plan to provide government that was representative of all its voting age citizens.

One day, our school bus picked us up on our regular morning bus stop. Instead of going to Boyle to the B.L. Bell Elementary School for classes, our driver, Mr. Friday, pulled the big yellow dog into the graveled parking area of the Hole in the Wall. He turned the bus around and said we were headed to the Bolivar County Expo for a field trip where we would meet up with our teachers.

As he drove up South Chrisman Avenue Extension, past the Hurricane Club, Mrs. Margie's Store, the old 400 Club site, the grave yard, Uncle Charles' junk yard, the Fairmans' home, Mr. Bob's Auto Shop, Nell's Barber Shop, the Swing Inn and the Myers' Store, but just before reaching Glassco Street, there were big orange and white construction caution blocks obstructing our passage. Beyond the detour sign and all along Glassco and in abutting areas of its perpendicular streets, we saw what appeared to be an endless row and piles of huge concrete pipes and super heavy-duty dirt-moving equipment. Workers were all about. Most of them wore white and grey striped uniforms that were stamped on the back with the words "Property of the Mississippi State Penitentiary (Parchman Prison Farm)." They were shoveling dirt and clearing debris from the big grudge ditch.

Mr. Friday pulled the bus to a stop before turning right to head up to U.S. 61 where he would then make a left turn and proceed on the highway to the County Expo Building. He turned to us with a big grin on his face. Shaking his head, he said, "Umph, umph, umph. Now that they are covering that grudge ditch, I don't know what I am going to call you all."

Acknowledgements

This book could not have been written without the love, care and guidance given by the many people who nourished and protected the children of the Grudge Ditch Gang. Mr. James "DeBoy" Carter, his wife Mrs. Margie Randle Carter and their children, Mr. J.W. Foster, his wife Mrs. Inez Foster and their children, Mr. Herman Johnson, the children and families of the Townsends, Williams, Randles, Ramseys, Winters, Walkers, Blocks, Fairmans, Searcys, Washingtons, Moores and many, many others who made up or helped to guide the Grudge Ditch Gang remain in my heart as part of my second family.

Commendations should surely go to the people who quietly and sometimes loudly fought for all Cleveland area adult residents to have voting rights and for the community to have basic services such as sanitation and water. They were taking care of our community while many of us younger children went around without a care in the world. Mrs. Fannie Lou Hamer, Mr. Amzie Moore, Mr. Roosevelt Grenell, the Rev. Dr. Martin Luther King, Jr., and many others gave much of their lives to something that I didn't know I needed, but they knew was critical for my future and the future of all children – that was, tearing down the walls of economic and racial discrimination.

The many children, risking bodily harm and death as they stood along side Mrs. Hamer in the struggle for freedom and equal rights, are my heroes, too. Joetha Collier, the Drew High School student, whose life was taken on the day of her high school graduation by a senseless shooting, all in the name of hate, continues to be a reminder to me about the brevity of life and the inevitable deadliness of the poisonous disease called hate.

Our pastor, the Rev. Sammie Lee Rash, provided many of the Grudge Ditch Gang with the spiritual guidance that helped us survive the tumultuous times of injustice, poverty and social unrest.

There has been much encouragement from many of my friends and as much patience as I told them, year after year, that I was going to write this book. Topping the list are Evelyn Fontenot, Alberta Jones, Phyllis Geans, Catherine Rimmer, Patricia Avery, Rojene Bailey, Josephine Clerk, Clair Askew, Josephine Smith, Franklin

Wesley, Georgia Antoine, Bernice Davis, Gerald Jones, Annette Tardy Morgan, Stanley Lee, Nettie Darden Leonard Brown, Naomia Wade, Melvin Latham, Lawanda Finney, Larry Tolliver, Tai Chatman, Terry Taylor, Joe Rogers, Eugheia Simon and Sandra Henson.

Despite my procrastination, several more of my friends suffered with me through the writing of "The Grudge Ditch Gang" by reading my rough drafts and continuing to encourage me. They – Donna Guillory, Sybil Comeaux, Shirley Bonton, Jolene Ortego, Marcia Greene, Carol Matthews, Gabby Polk, Linda Thomas, Carolyn Brown and Dora Nisby, as well as my "sister-cousins" Rhonda Williams Spann, Linda Spears and Gloria Jean Garrett – are most appreciated for laboring with and pushing me forward to write more and more and better and better. Every other vice got in my way – shopping, dining, playing, travelling, my job that keeps a roof over my head – and yet, these ladies accepted no excuse. They went beyond pushing and encouraging me to giving their own time to proof, edit and offer suggestions of improvements.

Of course, my teachers throughout school and my early writing career as a news reporter deserve credit for helping to develop the writer in me. Among them are Ernestine Bibbs, Ada Jackson, Dorothy Grenell, college professors Dr. Sabetha Jenkins and Dr. Gene Wiggins, along with *Delta Democrat-Times Newspaper* leaders Sallie Gresham, Philip Carter, Lynn Lafoe, Hodding

Carter, III, and others. They each helped me to hone my writing skills.

In just one meeting, several members of the Houston Chapter of the International Association of Business Communicators (IABC) and the Houston Writers Guild confirmed the thoughts of my longtime friends and family members that "The Grudge Ditch Gang" is a story that must be told. They, without the years of personal ties as held with my friends (whom I sometimes thought were just being nice and doing what friends are supposed to do), encouraged me even more to move forth with getting "The Grudge Ditch Gang" to market.

The Favre family opened their rural lakefront Mississippi farm and ranch to me. The peace and quiet away from telephones and televisions got me back on the right path to writing and helped me as I finally took time to deal with the deaths of my parents. The stories that tumbled forth had me falling to the floor laughing out loud or curling up in one of the big comfortable chairs crying as my mind recalled many of the painful or humorous episodes of being a child among the Haynes family. These are the stories of "The Grudge Ditch Gang" that served as healing balm to my mourning heart as they poured forth to my laptop and onto paper back in the woods of rural Southern Mississippi.

Then, just a few months later, a good friend and head of the Huggins family would not let me continue to put off finishing the Huckleberry Finn-like tales of my childhood that I had put to paper but still needed to fine tune. The Huggins' vacation home provided me more inspiration from nature's beautiful lakes, ponds, rolling hills and starry skies. It was there that I finally wrote and completed the last details of "The Grudge Ditch Gang."

I look back over my life and remember many times asking God why didn't He make me rich. Now, I know that He did. He made me rich with family, community and love. He gave me a great family. Grandmama Estella Haynes Vassar who died at the age of 102 was always a solid rock in my life and deserves a book all on her own. My sisters Sandra, Toni, Florida Rena, Phyllis and Malinda Jean and my brothers Randy, Samuel, Lester, Philip, Terry, Charles and Lawrence (along with the belatedly discovered youngest brother Dennis) are owed the deepest appreciation. These stories are theirs as well as mine.

Winnie Lee "Muddear" Haynes and Lawrence Douglas "L.D., Doctor Soul, Daddy" Haynes, who have gone on to glory, are owed all the gratitude a heart can muster. They believed in family, the core family being at our home there in the Low End, with concentric circles of family extending to our neighbors, the town of Cleveland and on to our family network across the globe – this worldwide family called mankind. While my parents are now deceased, people still come by our home on Chrisman Avenue Extended to visit and reminisce how "Mr. L.D. and Mrs. Winnie" impacted their lives.

Like pioneers, my parents took the risk of moving their family to a new community that they would join in as leaders to help develop. They managed to raise their children and help to raise many others in the face of civil unrest, poverty, politics and more. They never gave up on their children, nor did they give up on our community – Cleveland's Low End and home of the Grudge Ditch Gang.

Finally and most importantly, I thank God.

Afterword

The Grudge Ditch Gang II, due to on the presses in 2013, serves up stories about the next phase of how the Low End community in Cleveland, Mississippi, impacts Jessie's life through high school and college. In the meantime, many fans who got a sneak preview of the draft of this book, *The Grudge Ditch Gang*, found themselves thirsty for more. What happened to the community, what happened to our parents, where are all the members of the "gang" and a litany of other seemingly endless questions filled my in box of voice and e-mails. Readers will have to check out *The Grudge Ditch Gang II* to get many of those answers.

In the meantime, the bullet points that follow offer some insight.

1. The Grudge Ditch – Using prison labor, the grudge ditch was finally cleared of the remaining open sewage. Concrete pipes were laid to connect the sewer system and Glassco Street was widened and paved, covering the pipes and the once famous Grudge Ditch. Throughout the 1960s and even into the 1980s, in other towns across the Mississippi Delta, residents continued to struggle with this unhealthy way of life. One of the Delta's open sewer communities was located just a few miles north of Cleveland on U.S. Highway 61 became internationally renown. That was "Sugar Ditch" in Tunica, Mississippi. Acres and acres of cotton fields that surrounded Tunica were sold for development of the casino industry. As casinos were built, the sugar ditches of the Tunica area communities were demolished. The decrepit, deplorable shacks and open ditches of waste were replaced with federally aided construction of new homes. These homes are connected to real sewer operations that help to protect the health and safety of the residents in the area. While poverty reined very high in the Delta, even as sharecropping ended and casino operations tookover over the cotton industry, Tunica and many other Delta counties are still among the poorest counties in America.

2. Mrs. Fannie Lou Townsend Hamer – People say it is all about the dash. Mrs. Hamer's dash is between 1917 and 1977, her birth and death years. "I am sick and tired of being sick and tired" is the mantra made famous by Mrs. Hamer, who was the first cousin of our neighbor, Mrs. Margie Townsend Randle Carter. Freedom Summer 1964 highlighted much of Mrs. Hamer's work in voter registration drives that resulted in many Americans marching and dying to help the disenfranchised gain the right to vote. She organized protests, drives and information meetings, worked for the Student Non-violent Coordination Coalition and led a group of 68 delegates called the Mississippi Freedom Democratic Party to the Democratic National Convention in Atlantic City. Her work helped to change the face of Mississippi and the nation's political structure.

Across the South, sit-ins, marches and protests were going on to try to bring about equal opportunities in fair housing, health care, employment, education and voting. Freedom rides from the North to Southern towns, especially to towns in the Mississippi Delta, started in 1961. In 1962, James Meredith integrated the University of Mississippi under the protection of federal marshals. In 1963, Civil Rights activist Medgar Evers was murdered in front of his home in Jackson, Mississippi. Dr. Martin Luther King, Jr.'s, winning of the Nobel Peace Prize was preceded by the murder of American Civil Rights workers James Chaney, Andrew Goodman and Michael Schwerner. They were assassinated by members of the Klu Klux

Klan in Philadelphia, Mississippi, just a couple of hours Southeast of our home. The bloodshed continued across the South, including the death of Dr. King in 1968 when an assassin's bullet ended the Civil Rights leader's life just 90 minutes away from the Grudge Ditch community – on the balcony of the Lorraine Motel. There, Dr. King was about to rest from his efforts to help Memphis, Tennessee, sanitation workers get equal pay. Mrs. Hamer continued her involvement in the struggle for civil rights for all people until her death from complications of diabetes and other health issues in 1977.

Just after the emancipation from slavery and during Reconstruction, Mississippi elected the nation's first black U.S. senator – Hiram Revels. His senatorship was short-lived, but the multi-racial Revels, in the post Civil War era of the late 1800s, became the first president of what is now Alcorn State University, one of the nation's premiere historically black colleges (located just two hours South of Cleveland). Decades later, during Mrs. Hamer's time, with the exception of the all-black town of Mound Bayou, Mississippi, where I and many of my siblings were born in the Taborian Hospital, black-elected officials in Mississippi were few and far in between. The black vote was diluted, gerrymandered, poll-taxed and stunted everyway possible to deny Mississippi Deltans of color and African Americans all across the South the right to vote. The Civil Rights Act passed in 1964 and the

Voting Rights Act followed in 1965. In subsequent years, Mississippi earned the distinction of being the state with the most black elected officials per capita than any other state.

(Decades later, as I have lived in several states, friends often remark about me growing up in a racially violent Mississippi and how they will never consider living in or travelling to the Magnolia state. I find myself reminding them that I never saw a Klan rally until I lived in Pennsylvania and Virginia, that the pain of hangings and dragging of bodies are as fresh today here in Texas as they were in the 1960s in Mississippi. That police beatings of a Rodney King in California or immigrants in New York or youngsters in Beaumont, Texas, are just as deplorable as the racial hatred permeating the Civil Rights struggles of the 1960s. Then, I find myself telling them that they need to be thankful of Mississippians especially and all the people who fought, struggled, took a stand and faced jail, dogs, water hoses, violence, death and other persecutions so all of us still living this day and the children of the future could have real opportunities in the pursuit of life, liberty and happiness.)

3. Alley Bats – More famous in Cleveland, Mississippi, than the Grudge Ditch Gang was a group called the Alley Bats by some and Alley Backs by others. In the end, we all hung out with each other, considering we all went to the same high school and, consequently, played on the same sports teams and rooted for each other.

The downtown Cleveland area that was a community located behind the alley that was behind the main streets of Cleveland, was known as the home of the Alley Bats. In researching why my now friends and my one time formerly perceived enemies were called Alley Bats, I was told over and over that the youth of this community fought like bats. At the drop of a hat or of a word spoken, many of the youth had no problem biting, scratching, cutting, hitting or doing whatever they felt necessary to protect themselves, their family and/or their turf.

This community had little or no electricity. Their homes were lit by coal oil or kerosene lamps. The dirt roadway in front of their wood-frame row or shotgun houses and shacks were places few who didn't live in that community would be caught after nightfall. While the issues of the Grudge Ditch Gang may have focused on the open sewer in our community, the parents in the Alley Bat community had equally poignant concerns that impacted their daily lives as they worked to shelter, educate and provide for their families.

The alleys of downtown Cleveland no longer exist and consequently, the back roads of the alleys have disappeared, too. The neighborhood now is made of paved streets with affordable new brick homes, dotted with lawns that have shrubbery and flowers – a 1,000 percent contrast to the old Alley Backs or Alley Bats' community.

4. Terry Haynes – My brother Terry got to see the world after enlisting in the U.S. Navy. He later lived in California, worked for the U.S. Postal Service where he moved up the ranks and retired after leading part of the Houston region of the USPS. He opened his own manufacturing firm where he developed machinery to lift mail onto conveyor belts for distribution. He named the equipment after his loved ones, including our parents, such as the L.D. 400 or the W.L. 2000. With a son, a daughter and two grandchildren, Terry spends much of his time developing his company and chasing that little white ball on the golf course.

5. Malinda Jean Haynes – the oldest daughter of my parents died at the age of 55 after living with breast cancer for more than 20 years and suffering from heart disease. She and the love of her life, Finley, gave birth to their daughter Stacie and son Rodric. Before her death, she got to experience the joy of being a grandmother, recording a gospel record and living in Michigan and California before returning home to help take care of our ailing parents. Her daughter Stacie now lives in the home Malinda made in Shaw.

Her son served in the U.S. Army. He died in his late 30s, in the midst of his third tour in the Iraq War. (The family believes that Rodric encountered and was a victim of chemical warfare. In just weeks after passing a full battery of health exams that cleared him to return to Iraq, Rodric became suddenly ill with a fast growing, organ-attacking, aggressive cancer that took his life.) The Iraq War was later deemed unnecessary because the weapons of mass destruction that Iraq's leader Sadaam Hussein was accused of having were never found. Malinda's granddaughter and Rodric's daughter Jaisha became my daughter as I raised her during her last year of high school.

Whether the DDT pesticide that was sprayed throughout the Delta was part of why Malinda suffered from breast cancer and had to have a double mastectomy in her early 30s remains unclear. There were many studies conducted in the post 1960s indicating the possibilities of the pesticide being the cause of wide spread cancer in the Mississippi Delta.

6. Philip Haynes – My brother, who scared the daylights out of me as the cesspool monster made his home in California. He joined the military but was discharged after a short stint for an injury he received during service. Philip died at the age of 33 from colon cancer. An avid tennis player, Philip was the no-nonsense brother who after leaving Mississippi vowed to never return. He didn't until his death. His body is now buried in the cemetery located just across the street from our family home on Chrisman Avenue Extended in Cleveland. Not only did Philip die from colon cancer, so did a couple of his classmates and later so did our father die at the age of 80 of colon and stomach cancer. Again, many of my siblings and relatives wondered if the cotton pesticides played a role in their demise.

7. Grandmama Estella Mobley Haynes Vassar – Grandmama died in 2002 at the age of 101. She built her own home with her own hands, raised her own foods and was constant in caring for us. In her late 80s, Grandmama was still physically healthy, but mental deterioration started infiltrating her mind via Alzheimer's Disease. By the time she was 90, Grandmama had to be cared for in a nursing home. Once a beautiful healthy size 14 (just like Marilyn Monroe), nearly six feet tall with thick healthy hair that hung down her back, I visited Grandmama on her 101st birthday in the nursing home. She was folded into a fetal position, was barely skin and bones (maybe a size 0) and all of her beautiful hair had been cut down to a few inches to be more manageable for the nursing home staff.

The many secrets she shared about where she buried her money were long forgotten by me. All I know is if anyone ever dug up her garden or went inside the walls of her home, they should have hit a few jackpots! She was a strong, independent, intelligent, interesting and exciting woman. In her mid-80s, Grandmama, who had buried two husbands, was dating a 45-year-old man! While Daddy didn't like her new love, Grandmama probably was the original "cougar."

8. Florida Randle – one of my best childhood friends, still lives in Cleveland. She dabbles in real estate and is a mother and grandmother now. After I went off to college at the University of Southern Mississippi in Hattiesburg, my neighbor Florida, as well as my cousin Rosemary joined me there. Rosemary earned her degree in fashion design and then started her career as an officer in the U.S. Air Force. Florida was so committed to wanting to be a teacher, that she became the first college graduate of Mrs. Margie and Mr. DeBoy's family. Even in the late 1970s, about a decade after sneaking off to march with her "Cousin Fannie Lou," Florida continued in carrying America's torch toward equal opportunity by earning her degree in teaching!

9. The Hole in the Wall Nightclub – One day, much into the new millennium, I sat in my den watching the Public Broadcasting Station (PBS). Low and behold, there appeared a documentary on the little nightclub that was located at the end of South Chrisman Avenue Extended in Cleveland, Mississippi. The building no longer stands but the artists and musicians the nightclub helped to establish have left their marks on a very important world culture – the blues! I know for a fact, it was the soothing music of the blues that helped Daddy and so many Mississippi Deltans survive the personal and corporate struggles they faced. Every time I hear the song "Down Home Blues" or "My Baby Wants to Go to the Hole in the Wall," not only do I want dance and sing, but I am warmly reminded of the many weekends I, my siblings and members of the Grudge Ditch Gang swept, mopped and picked up trash at the one and only, original "Hole in the Wall."

10. Muddear and Daddy – Daddy died at age 80 in 2002 after being diagnosed with stomach and colon cancer. Muddear died eight years later at the age of 84, suffering mostly from diabetes and heart disease. In his retirement years, Daddy's hobby of music became more and more important to him. His title of "Dr. Soul" was relevant as he used his music to help heal the heartaches and pain suffered by many of the residents of the Delta. Muddear, unlike Tyler Perry's MaDea, continued to quietly share her recipes of love and patience to all who came her way.

Married for more than 60 years, my parents meant the world to the Grudge Ditch Gang. For me, all my siblings, and young people from all across Cleveland, there was one purpose we wanted to achieve most in life –that was and continues to be "to make our parents proud."

Order Items from Jessie Haynes Books Today!

Expected *Grudge Ditch Gang* Release Date: **September 1, 2012**
All pre-orders received by December 15, 2012 will receive FREE shipping and a 10% price discount *(does not include e-books)*

LIST OF ITEMS: Price each	Quantity	Total
1. The Grudge Ditch Gang - Hardcover - book - **$21.95**	_____	_______
2. The Grudge Ditch Gang - Paperback - book - **$16.95**	_____	_______
3. The Grudge Ditch Gang - Audio book on CD - **$14.99**	_____	_______
4. The Grudge Ditch Gang - E reader version - **$9.99** *(available online at the special promotional price from October 1 - December 15, 2012 on iTunes, Amazon.com & Kindle.com)*	_____	_______
5. Ten Stupid Things College Kids Do - **$8.95**	_____	_______
6. The Grudge Ditch Gang mug - **$7.99**	_____	_______
7. The Grudge Ditch Gang t-shirt - **$10.99**	_____	_______
8. The Grudge Ditch Gang cap - **$9.99**	_____	_______
Subtotal		_________
10% Discount *(Pre-orders before December 15, 2012)*		_________
After December 15, 2012, shipping/handling: $2.50 per item *(delivery within 7-10 days)*		_________
Tax: 8.25% *(applicable for orders in the state of Texas)*		_________

Name ______________________ Address ______________________________

City ______________________________ State _____ Zip ______________

Phone ______________________ email ______________________________

Autographed copies to: Name(s)

______________________ ______________________

______________________ ______________________

______________________ ______________________

______________________ ______________________

______________________ ______________________

Payment Options:

Credit Card # ______________________________ Security Code ___________

Expiration Date ________________ Signature ______________________

Check or money order enclosed: $ ________ amount enclosed

Fill out this form and mail in with payment. Makes checks payable to:
The Advanced Marketing Team • P.O. Box 22577 • Beaumont, TX 77720-2577
visit our website: ***www.jessiehaynesbooks.com***

Reserve your copy of the next book by Jessie Haynes...
Diary of a PR Woman...due out later in 2013